THE YOUNG
CITIZEN'S READER

THE YOUNG CITIZEN'S READER

by

Paul Reinsch

updated by

Lisa M. Ripperton

YESTERDAY'S CLASSICS

ITHACA, NEW YORK

This edition, first published in 2017 by Yesterday's Classics, an imprint of Yesterday's Classics, LLC, is an updated version of the text originally published by Benjamin H. Sanborn & Company in 1909, with a substantial amount of new material describing the state of affairs in the 21st century. For the complete listing of the books that are published by Yesterday's Classics, please visit www.yesterdaysclassics.com. Yesterday's Classics is the publishing arm of the Baldwin Online Children's Literature Project which presents the complete text of hundreds of classic books for children at www.mainlesson.com.

ISBN: 978-1-63334-091-6

Yesterday's Classics, LLC
PO Box 339
Ithaca, NY 14851

INTRODUCTION

Young persons are not alone in preferring to see how things are done in political life rather than to study the bare legal framework of the state. The author believes that emphasis on the structure of our government has been carried too far, especially in books for children and young students. The subject has been given too much of a legal character. Now to see people at work, to see them struggling for influence and power and performing the duties of office and of citizenship, is undoubtedly far more interesting than to consider the underlying legal principles of constitutional organization. The writer of this little book, the result of a period of leisure from more exacting duties, has therefore attempted to make it a portrayal of action in political life. Its prime purpose is to train boys and girls to notice and to understand what is going on about them in their town, state, and nation. However, for intelligent action in matters of politics, we need also some understanding of the outward form of government. After the more essential methods of political action have been described, some attention will therefore be given to the structure of the state in all its parts. To the ordinary citizen it is far more important to understand the meaning of such matters as elections, the action of the city council, and the police, than to dwell upon the refinements of constitutional law. Only the most essential features of state organization have therefore been pointed out.

Politics and government are human action — life and action of the most interesting kind. They are action, moreover, upon which our personal welfare and happiness are directly dependent. We cannot be members of a state in which corruption and injustice govern without feeling the bad results in our own life. The life of a state is our life written large. Without a well-arranged and orderly state life, complete private happiness is not possible. Moreover, there is no satisfaction in life so great as devotion to the welfare of the state. All private satisfaction seems small when compared with that of a citizen who has gained the confidence of fellow-citizens through honest action and personal sacrifice.

There is such a multitude of facts in connection with political life that it is necessary to select those which are most important for young Americans to know. A small book like this cannot pretend to be complete. If we should try to fill it with a description of every political institution, it would become a dreary catalogue of things that mean nothing to our minds. But while we cannot cover the ground completely, we can endeavor to point out those things which are most vital and important, in order that they may acquire a meaning in the minds of young persons which will help them much in after life. This is not a handbook on American government, but only the first introduction into that fascinating field.

INTRODUCTION

Institutions differ so much in different parts of our country that some of them can be described only in general terms. It is for the young students themselves to see what particular form an institution takes in their own community and neighborhood. To make them find out these things by inquiry and observation is the best training that their minds can receive. People should be able to see for themselves and interpret the meaning of what is going on around them. For this reason there have been added to each chapter a few questions to be answered by the pupil after inquiry and observation. These are, of course, only in the nature of suggestions to the teacher. The information is not to be taken from books, but is to be obtained through personal inquiry. The intelligent use of newspaper information [and trusted internet sources, too], may be taught in this connection. Often these questions will be designed also to train the judgment in that they will call for a decision between two alternatives. The study of political action offers a rare opportunity for training the power of observation as well as the judgment. As in the natural sciences, a pupil must learn to observe accurately and to judge what he sees. It is apparent that a republic is especially in need of citizens who are able to do their own thinking, and to see the real through the veil of outward appearances.

P. S. R.

The University of Wisconsin,

January, 1909.

CONTENTS

Part III. The Organization of the Government

Part IV. Some American Ideals

Part V. Federal Documents

PART I

The Government
and the Citizen

CHAPTER I

THE TRUE NATURE
OF GOVERNMENT

Government in Early Times. — Wherever people live together in communities, government exists. It has, however, very different forms. Among the isolated peoples in Africa, Asia, and South America, the communities are typically very small. They have at their head a chieftain. As isolation decreases, a number of such communities or tribes are brought together under the power of a single ruler. In the earlier stages of community life there is apt to be much warfare. War demands obedience on the part of the army to its commander. So it comes about that the head of the state at times when war is common becomes very powerful. As the power passes from generation to generation, certain families establish their authority for long periods. Such royal families, whose history goes back to these early warlike times, still exist in a few countries, like England and Sweden. In some of these countries, however, the power of the sovereign has been greatly limited; while in a number of countries such as the United States, France, and Switzerland, no sovereign family exists at all, the government being carried on by persons elected by the citizens in general.

In earlier times government was looked upon as something imposed from above. The royal power seemed so strong that there was no possibility of resisting it. Kings and queens often claimed that they exercised divine power. In such periods the people were not supposed to do anything but obey commands given from above. A state with such a government has an unstable foundation. As it would be unsafe to build a house upon a foundation narrower than the house itself, so a state which rests only on a small number of people is not secure. It is far better that the power of all the people should be recognized in order that the state may have their intelligent support.

Government in Modern Times. — In our own times a government that should rely on force alone would have no security among an intelligent people. Our idea of government is different. The government is merely the people acting directly or through its agents and representatives, for their own benefit. We cannot live happily unless we are willing to obey reasonable laws which protect the life and property of ourselves as well as of others. We need the company and assistance of other people. We need schools, churches, universities, business associations, societies, and clubs of various kinds. In order that we may be able to enjoy all these advantages of social life, we must also observe the rules laid down for social action. In order that these rules may be just and reasonable and impartially enforced, we elect certain of our fellow-citizens to make laws or

4

to appoint officials for their execution. When we obey these laws and officers, we are simply obeying what we ourselves consider just and right.

The Real Government. — The government is composed of the individuals whom the people elect to office, together with officers who are appointed by them under the law. These persons do the work in which all citizens are interested. They ought, therefore, to consider the welfare and interest of all members of the state. The government is not something apart from our life, something outside of us, set over us; it is simply ourselves, the people, acting for our common benefit. The persons whom we intrust with power do not have any special privilege, nor should they look upon their office as a source of advantage to themselves. We have given them influence and authority in order that they may do the work in which we are all interested. An official, no matter how high, is under the law just as any other citizen. Thus, if a governor or a president should violate the speed laws on a public road, he or she would be subject to arrest and fine like any other citizen. The power of an individual is only such as the law has prescribed, and is no greater than that individual's responsibilities.

We need faithful, unselfish public servants who really think of and work for what is best for the community, that is, for all of us. Such persons we shall honor and reward for their honesty and efficiency. In individuals who use their office simply to benefit themselves or their friends, we shall have no confidence. If they consider what is good for any small group of persons or for any corporation rather than for the people as a whole, they are not faithful servants of the public. They are servants of the few — of individuals who possibly reward them with private gain, while we, the public, are ignored as of no importance. We shall not trust persons in office when we discover that their character is not that of honest public servants.

QUESTIONS

1. Are you a citizen? Of what? Tell the difference between a citizen and a voter.

2. What is a monarchy? An oligarchy? A plutocracy? A democracy?

3. How far back can you trace the family of Queen Elizabeth II?

4. What is a corporation? A republic? An ordinance?

5. Why should we obey city ordinances?

6. What is patriotism? How can boys and girls show their patriotism?

7. Name some public officials in your city or town. Were they elected or appointed, and by whom?

8. How does the government of the United States differ from that of England?

CHAPTER II

THE CITIZEN'S PART
IN GOVERNMENT

A Pure Democracy. — While the work of government is carried on by elected and appointed officials who represent the people, the citizens themselves have important duties to fulfill in connection with the public business. There are some small communities in which the citizens themselves directly perform almost the entire work of governing. In the mountain regions of Switzerland there are cantons or communities in which all the citizens meet once or several times a year to discuss all matters of common interest. On these occasions they vote for laws and regulations and instruct the permanent officials as to how they are to conduct public affairs. In our country we have a similar institution in the *town meeting* found in New England, in New York, and in several Western commonwealths, in which the citizens of a town come together to discuss matters relating to the common welfare. They vote on the raising of money, on the building and repair of roads, on school business, and similar matters. They elect some of their number, often called *selectmen*, to carry

7

their votes into effect and transact business connected therewith. We call this form of public action *direct democracy.* Democracy is a Greek word meaning the rule of the people. In the town the people rule directly. They make their own by-laws and regulations without electing representatives for that purpose.

A Representative Government. — But it is plain that in a large city, in a state, or in a nation, it would be impossible to have all the citizens meet together for discussion and voting. A mass meeting of several thousand or a hundred thousand people is wholly impracticable. It is therefore necessary that smaller groups within the city or state — say wards or districts in the city or towns and counties in the state — should select representatives to meet together as a council or legislature to make laws and regulations for the government of the community. In a nation like our own the most important duty of the citizens, therefore, is that of voting. When the citizen casts his ballot, he decides who is to represent him in the exercise of power. The people not only select the persons who are to hold office, but they also control the policies of public action which are to be followed, because candidates for office always declare what policies they stand for. The citizens or electors therefore choose not only between individuals but between policies.

Intelligent Voting. — Many people do not realize the importance of the act they perform when they cast their ballots. There are even people who do not think for themselves when they are voting, but follow the advice of others. All citizens should know what candidates they want to vote for as the best representatives of their idea of the public good. They should inquire about them, and find out whether in offices which they may have formerly held they have been honest and efficient. They should read their arguments and see what policies they support. If they find that they are not to be trusted, or that they support wrong policies, they should not vote for them.

We see that there are many things to inquire about before voting. It is, therefore, better that there should not be too many elective offices. Let the most important officers be elected by the people, but let all other officials be appointed. If we have to vote for a large number of offices, we cannot often vote intelligently. We cannot learn all we ought to know about the individual candidates before the election. If, however, we vote only for persons to fill the most important positions, we may ordinarily do so wisely, and may thus control the policy of the entire government, the subordinate officials being dependent in their action.

Admission to Citizenship. — All persons born in the United States are American citizens, no matter what the nationality of their parents may be. People from other countries who are lawful permanent residents of the United States may apply for citizenship.

QUESTIONS

1. What is the difference between a direct democracy and a representative democracy?

2. What are cantons? By-laws? A constitution? Selectmen?

3. Which form of government is better in a place of fifteen thousand inhabitants? Why?

4. Who is at the head of the government in the place of your residence? Are his or her assistants appointed or elected?

5. Give four names applied to the presiding officer of a meeting.

6. What is a ward or district? How many in your city?

7. What is a county? How constituted? How many in your state?

8. What is the most important duty that a citizen has to perform? Why?

9. Should a citizen vote for a candidate for office or for the policies which the candidate represents? Why?

10. What is a town meeting? Where found? What matters are voted upon?

11. What steps must a person born in another country take to become a citizen of the United States?

CHAPTER III

NOMINATIONS

Selecting Candidates for Office. — In the election one may, of course, vote for any citizen whom one desires to place in office. It is customary, however, for voters to name or nominate certain candidates before the election, because otherwise the votes would be scattered. One would not care to throw away one's vote by casting it for a person whom no one else puts on his ballot. Citizens, therefore, combine to select a person for whom they will vote. In this way parties are formed. *Political parties* are citizens within the state who stand for certain policies and who act together in nominating officials to carry out those policies.

Nominating Process. — The process of nominating candidates to stand for public office at the local, state, and national levels varies from one state to another and from one party to another.

For the presidency the nomination process consists of two types of elections held at the state level — primaries and caucuses — followed by a national convention.

Primaries. — In a primary, voters go to a local

polling place and vote by secret ballot for their preferred candidate from a slate of candidates. The number of votes each candidate receives determines the number of delegates that candidate will have at their party's convention.

Caucuses. — Caucuses are private meetings run by political parties. In most, participants divide themselves into groups according to the candidate they support, with undecided voters forming into a group of their own. Each group then gives speeches supporting its candidate and tries to persuade others to join its group. At the end of the caucus, party organizers count the voters in each candidate's group and calculate how many delegates each candidate has won.

Conventions. — After the primaries and caucuses, most political parties hold national conventions to finalize their choice for Presidential and Vice Presidential nominees. The national conventions typically confirm the candidate who has already won the required number of delegates through the primaries and caucuses. However, if no candidate has received the majority of a party's delegates, the convention becomes the stage for choosing that party's Presidential nominee.

QUESTIONS

1. Do you have primaries or caucuses in your state?

2. At the next primary election let your parent show you a ballot, or go online to see a sample ballot. See how many candidates are named on this ballot.

3. What is the meaning of primary? Politics? Nominate? Try to find the origin of the word "candidate."

4. Which is more important, the nomination or the election of an official?

5. What is a political party? Name four.

6. What is a convention? What does the word "convention" mean?

7. Who is entitled to vote in a primary?

8. For what offices were candidates voted for in the last primary in your town?

CHAPTER IV

ELECTIONS

Voting by Ballot. — With us, elections are carried on entirely by *ballot;* that is, by a vote written or printed upon a slip or sheet of paper, or recorded on a voting machine. A ballot includes the names of the candidates of all parties, with the candidates of each party typically printed in a separate column. A person desiring to vote for all the candidates of one party can mark the box at the head of that party column. But a person desiring to vote for candidates from different parties can mark the box next to the name of each candidate for whom he or she wishes to vote.

Voting Machines. — Voting machines are in use in many states. These machines save the trouble of marking a ballot, while counting and registering the number of votes cast for every candidate.

The Process of Voting. — Elections are held in local polling places. Representatives of the local election board staff each polling place to verify the registration of voters as they enter. Once verified, the voter receives a ballot (if paper ballots are used) and proceeds to the voting booth. On entering the voting booth, the voter marks his or her ballot. After carefully looking it over to see that no mistake has been made, the voter deposits it in the ballot-box. If there is a voting machine, the voter will pull certain levers or press certain buttons which will register his or her vote. Each party is entitled to have election observers present at each polling place to ensure fairness of the proceedings.

Whether the voter casts his or her vote by paper ballot or by machine, the vote is secret, and nobody knows who has been favored. At the present time one is not obliged to make one's vote public, though most persons are independent enough to tell frankly whom they have supported. Some people think that it is a disgrace to have voted for a candidate who has been defeated; but if the voter acts intelligently and honestly, defeat does not matter. The majority is sometimes wrong. It is better to feel that one is right with a few than wrong with the majority.

Political Campaigns. — Preceding the election, the candidates urge upon the voters their claims to office. A campaign really is a series of military movements and battles in a war. As we have substituted the ballot for force, we have freed ourselves from the need of battles to determine who the rulers shall be; but we call a political contest a campaign because citizens can fight with speeches and ballots as well as with arms. Careful voters will make up their minds in their choice between different candidates on the basis of the principles they stand for and the service they have rendered. In this they are assisted by the arguments made during the campaign. These we sometimes call stump speeches, because when our country was new and but recently settled, many tree stumps were still left standing in village streets. It was very convenient for a candidate who wanted to address the villagers to mount one of these stumps and to make his speech from this point of vantage. If he became very profuse in cheap and insincere patriotism, it was said, "He made the eagle scream." Very often the campaign speeches took the form of deriding and blackening the character of the other party, or of telling jokes meant to ridicule the opposition. At present, campaigns have become more dignified. We like to hear a witty speaker who knows how to take advantage of the weaknesses of the other side, but we are not satisfied with ancient jokes and a superficial oratory. The most successful political orators today know that the great interests of the public, the important work that the government is doing, are more fascinating subjects than anything else on which a campaign speech can be made. They, therefore, speak to their audiences upon matters that are really worth while. They do not seek merely to amuse their hearers, but they appeal to their judgment.

Voting on Changes in the Constitution. — While citizens most frequently vote for public officials, they are also occasionally called on to express their choice regarding important matters of law or public expediency. This takes place when *constitutional amendments* are submitted to the people. A constitution is the body of law which lies at the basis of government. It fixes the general powers of officers and guarantees the rights of citizens. A change in the constitution, called an amendment, is the most important act of the citizens of a free state. The fundamental law upon which everything else depends is affected by such action. The proposed amendments will be printed at the bottom of the ballots or upon separate sheets. Upon these amendments the citizens vote either "yes" or "no." It is strange that usually the vote on amendments is very small as compared with the vote for officials. This shows that many people do not appreciate the importance of a change in the constitution. They do not take the time to inform themselves as to what the amendment means. For example, it may provide that the state shall be authorized to borrow money for the construction of public roads. Voters should consider whether it is advisable for the state to incur a debt for this purpose. They should consider how valuable good roads are to a commonwealth — how much they add in usefulness and enjoyment to the life of the citizens. Only after one has fully considered these matters and is fully informed should one cast one's vote.

Oversight of Officials. — We ought to know the business of the state or government because it is our own business and affects our own happiness. We should give heed to what the public servants are doing and how they are fulfilling their duties. We cannot expect that officials will be faithful to our interests if we do not reward them for honest action with our confidence. If we do not attend to our own affairs, nobody else will do it for us. We have a common proverb, "Mind your own business." This has often been falsely interpreted to mean that a person should confine himself exclusively to his or her own individual interests. It is, of course, very wise that we should not waste any attention on what concerns other people only. But when we go before the legislature and argue for the protection of forests or for the building of good roads, or when we tell the city council that no franchises should be given without proper return to the people and the city, we are attending to our own business; because, if these things are not settled in the right manner, we may personally suffer in consequence.

QUESTIONS

1. What is a "hand vote"? A "yea and nay vote"? A "roll-call vote"? A "*viva voce* vote"?

2. When may each of these ways of voting be used?

3. What is a ballot? Try to find the origin of the word.

4. Why are states sometimes called common-wealths?

5. What are some of the advantages of a secret ballot?

6. What are some of the advantages of a voting machine?

7. Find the meaning of guarantee; legislature; franchise; register.

CHAPTER V

SOME DUTIES OF CITIZENS

Office-holding. — The duty of the citizen is not fully done when one has voted for officials and on constitutional amendments. One may be called by one's fellow-citizens to hold public office oneself. In this case it is one's duty, even at some personal sacrifice, to undertake this work for the state and the community. Some offices do not require much attention. They are simply honorary and without salary. The office of presidential elector is such. In most cases, however, public office involves labor and time. It is, therefore, just that the public should pay its officers well, so that their loss may not be too great. We ought not to expect persons to leave their business and devote their time and thought and energy to the public without suitable remuneration. But in turn the office-holder should look upon oneself as a representative of the public. The value of one's position is not to be estimated by the privileges or income which it brings to oneself, but by the advantages which one can secure for the public by means of it. The highest honor in the world is public confidence, not a large income. The President of the United States is paid $400,000 a year. Its Chief

Justice receives $255,500, cabinet officers, $205,700, and senators and representatives, $174,000. Yet there are many millionaires who would willingly surrender their entire income in order to enjoy the public confidence which goes with these high offices.

Jury Service. — Another duty of citizens is to serve on juries in the trial of civil and criminal cases. For this service the citizen is given a small remuneration, but it is a duty which is often irksome and disagreeable. To sit through a long, tedious trial, perhaps for weeks, listening to testimony and the arguments of attorneys, and then to be confined with other jurors for hours, or even days, until the verdict has been agreed upon, is often a very undesirable experience. There is no duty of citizens, however, in the performance of which higher demands are made upon their character. All our laws rest upon the people. They must ultimately enforce them through juries in all parts of our country. When a person has committed a crime, that person ought to be punished. He or she should neither be persecuted in malice nor freed through pity. The *majesty* of the law must be upheld. Often when jurors see how a person has been led into temptation by others, how that person has failed through weakness of character, and how his or her spouse and innocent children will suffer through that person's imprisonment, they are moved with compassion, and it becomes a hard task to condemn the defendant. Yet it must be done, because punishment is meted out to offenders in order that the people may be protected. Upon the character and intelligence of jurors depend the enforcement of law and the security of the people.

Military Service. — All citizens of the state are under obligation to defend their country in case of need. Should our country be attacked from without, the citizen must be ready to come to its aid. At such a time one is merely standing up for the defense of one's home, one's family, and all that is dear to him or her. In times of war the government is given the right to compel the citizen to render military service. One may be drafted into the army, and must serve unless one's physical condition is such as to make it impossible. While, happily, our country is so powerful and in such friendly relations with other countries that war need not be feared, yet it is our duty to be ready at any time to enter the military and fight for the security of our country. We should train our bodies so that we can endure fatigue and hardship, otherwise the first experience in a military camp would make us helpless. Our nation will be strong if its citizens are healthy, vigorous, and able to defend themselves.

Payment of Taxes. — It is the duty of the citizen to be always ready and willing to contribute to the support of the government. When we consider all the benefits which come to us through the government, we should be willing to pay our share of its expenses. Unfortunately, some people, in one way or another, avoid the payment of their just part of the burden of taxation. In defrauding the state citizens defraud themselves, because if they do not want to carry the burdens, they cannot expect to share the privileges of good government.

QUESTIONS

1. What are the disadvantages of an official salary that is too small? Of one that is too large?

2. What are the salaries of some of your town or state officers?

3. How are jurors selected?

4. What persons are excused from jury service?

5. Is it proper for a candidate for office to advocate his or her own election?

6. Are "office-seekers" good citizens?

7. What qualities make a person a good juror? A good soldier? A good office-holder? A good citizen?

8. Is it worse to cheat your neighbor or to cheat the government?

9. Who should be excused from military service?

10. Does the same jury consider all kinds of cases? Why not?

11. What are jurors paid?

12. Who is the commander-in-chief of the United States army?

13. What is a tax? How are taxes levied?

14. Name three kinds of taxes.

15. What is an income tax? Is an income tax justifiable? Why?

PART II

What Governments Do

CHAPTER VI

MAINTAINING ORDER

Protection in Feudal Times. — We all desire to live in peace, to have our homes free from invasion, to have our property protected. Only thus may we work, travel, and play in comfort and peace. But who threatens the order under which we live? In earlier ages society was very insecure. Men desired to get what they could, and had little respect for one another's rights. So it was necessary for each man to protect his own by the force of his right arm. Sheltered locations were much sought after. Men preferred to build their homes on high and inaccessible rocks. When we stand on the ramparts of one of the castles in Scotland or on the Rhine, we realize what protection against injury meant in those early days. The man who had succeeded in building for himself a castle on an eminence, well protected with powerful walls and battlements, had not only secured safety for himself and family, but he could also give protection to the people of the neighborhood. On his watch-towers stood sentinels who could see a hostile force approaching from the distance. They could give warning to the peasants who were working in the fertile fields of the plains and valleys below. These would hurry with their wives and children up the road to the castle to seek protection within its walls. But, for the safety thus gained, they had given up their independence to the lord of the castle. They worked for him, they brought what grain they could produce and what cattle they could raise for his use, keeping only enough themselves to support a bare existence. Thus protection against violence is an advantage for which people have in many cases given up practically all they had.

Cities grew in this fashion. Athens, Corinth, Rome, — all the cities of antiquity — were built on precipitous hills. They had their acropolis, a word which means a steep city, a fortress on an inaccessible hill-top. There stood the temples in which the divinities of the city found their home. On the lower slopes and on the surrounding plains citizens lived, worked, and traded. But they could always take refuge within the protecting walls of the fortress. As their wealth and importance grew, they built outer fortress walls enclosing the entire settlement. In the Middle Ages all towns were walled in this fashion. The citizens thus protected could develop their rights of free government. The cities were the cradles of modern liberty. They could successfully defend themselves against long sieges; although when the force of the opponent was overpowering, they fell, their walls were broken down, and the city given over to massacre and destruction.

Protection against Individuals. — In our age people in general have a greater respect for one another's rights. Castles or city walls are no longer needed for protection. Nations, indeed, are still building powerful fortresses, but within their own territory mutual protection does not require castle walls. Castles are relics of a former civilization, interesting chiefly for their picturesqueness and for the beautiful views that can be enjoyed from their ramparts. We are protected by the general respect for the rights of life and property which pervade the entire community.

There are, however, still found in almost every community those who will violate the rights of others by theft, murder, or other crimes. These individuals have the instincts of an earlier time in the development of our civilization. They are a menace against which the state is under obligation to protect us. This work of protection is carried on by the police force and other officials who have police powers, such as sheriffs and constables in towns. The police should be constantly watchful to prevent crime and to make its punishment possible by the arrest of suspects. A police officer who falls asleep on his or her beat or spends time at places of amusement, where not stationed by orders of the chief, should be dismissed from the service. Criminal activity is lessened in cities where an efficient police force exists, but increased in towns where the police force is inefficient or corrupt. As protection against crime and violence is the first duty of the government, so no greater evil can exist than an alliance between the police and wrong-doers, through which wrong-doers are allowed to escape in return for a share in their ill-gotten gains. It seems impossible that such things can exist; and yet when citizens are not watchful, greed and corruption will sometimes bring about such deplorable conditions.

The Arrest of the Suspect. — When a police officer suspects that a crime has been committed, or that a person has broken the law, he should at once arrest the suspect. In a country district such arrest will usually be made by a sheriff or constable. To resist a peace officer is itself a crime, so that even if the arrest is illegal, no resistance should be made. If the officer is not able to handle the suspect or suspects alone, he or she may call in the assistance of any citizens present, and the latter are obliged to help in making the arrest or in pursuing the fleeing suspect. If one should see a crime committed, it is one's right and duty to arrest the suspect on the spot in order to prevent his or her escape. Here, too, we see that the agents of the government are only doing the work which we as citizens might do for ourselves, but which for convenience has been intrusted to some designated person. No citizen should, however, assume to judge and punish a wrong-doer outside of the regular courts.

Extradition. — Should a suspect escape into another state, a judge in the state where the crime was committed will issue an interstate arrest warrant. Once the suspect is arrested, the state where the crime was alleged to have been committed will ask to have the suspect extradited. *Extradition* means the handing over of an arrested person by one state to the authorities of another. Should large bodies of the population riot and destroy the property and endanger the lives of other citizens, the militia of the state may be called out to assist the peace officers; and when the legislature or governor of a state asks for it, United States troops in the form of the Army National Guard and the Air National Guard will be sent to help in restoring order. The militia and the troops should, however, be used only when actual violence is threatened and when the ordinary peace officers are plainly unable to restore order.

Trial of Defendants. — When a suspect has been arrested, his or her trial before a court of the state follows. The accused is first given a preliminary hearing before a magistrate, that is, a justice of the peace or a municipal judge. After it is found that good cause exists for his or her arrest, the accused will be bound over for trial. The magistrate, if the case is not one of murder, will ordinarily permit the accused to go free until the time of trial, if sufficient bail can be furnished. *Bail* may be described as a payment of money, or as a promise of such payment, to secure the appearance of an accused person at trial. If the accused should meanwhile escape and not appear when the trial begins, the money thus paid or promised would be forfeited to the state.

In criminal actions the state itself is the plaintiff. It is represented by the prosecuting attorney, who is usually called State's Attorney or District Attorney. He or she draws up the accusation against the accused in proper legal form. This must be done exceedingly carefully, because if the crime charged is not properly described, the action may fail and the accused may be dismissed by the court. When the day for trial comes, the accused is arraigned before the court. The defendant is asked whether he or she pleads guilty or not guilty to the charges. Should the accused plead guilty, that is, should he or she admit guilt openly, the judge will immediately pronounce judgment and fix the punishment under the law. If the defendant pleads not guilty, that is, denies guilt, the trial begins.

The Defense of the Defendant. — The accused is entitled to counsel. If the individual cannot afford to pay an attorney, the judge will appoint some one to defend him or her. Formerly, the accused was not permitted to bring any counsel into the court, and in general was treated as if guilty and had to prove his or her innocence. But it was found that many innocent persons were unjustly condemned and punished under this arrangement. In our country we have decided to give the accused every possible protection in order that one may clear oneself if one is not guilty. The defendant is allowed counsel. One need not testify against oneself, though one may testify in one's own favor. The defendant is presumed not to be guilty until his or her guilt is proven, and it must be proven so strongly that no reasonable doubt remains. If the defendant thinks the judge will be unfavorable to him or her, or that the entire neighborhood is strongly prejudiced, he or she may ask to have the case tried in some other county. This is called a *change of venue.* If the persons who have been drawn for the jury do not seem fair to him or her, the defendant may object to a certain number of them, and when the verdict and judgment have been finally given, it may be appealed to a higher court. Certainly the rights of an individual could not be protected more carefully than is done under our laws. It is unfortunate that improper advantage is taken of this liberality, and that scheming attorneys will sometimes shield the guilty by using many legal technicalities which our liberal system makes possible.

The Jury. — To return to the trial. The first thing after the accused has pleaded not guilty is to select a jury of twelve people to decide the question of his or her innocence or guilt. The sheriff or jury commissioners have prepared a list of jurors called a *panel*. These jurors are called up one by one by the clerk of the court. They are questioned as to whether they have any prejudice in the matter, and if neither the accused nor the state objects to a juror, the individual is sworn in by the clerk of the court, and takes his or her seat in the jury-box. When twelve jurors have thus been selected, the trial begins. Witnesses are examined, the attorneys make their arguments, and the judge instructs or *charges* the jury as to what law ought to be applied in the case. After this the jurors retire to a special room, where they hold their deliberations. They must agree before the verdict can be rendered. Sometimes they will sit through days and nights before they can come to a decision. If they are so hopelessly divided that they can never unite in their opinions, they will report to the court that they cannot render a verdict, and a new trial must take place. As a trial is expensive, it is always desirable that juries should give a verdict. When they have united on a verdict, they inform the judge, who calls the court together in the presence of the jury and prisoner. They then give the *verdict* of guilty or not guilty.

Evidence of Guilt. — The position of a juror is one of great responsibility. One should be absolutely

31

impartial, and not allow one's feelings to injure or favor the accused. While one will feel sympathy for the offender, one must remember that law and order can only be upheld by the punishment of criminals. If one has a reasonable doubt of the guilt of the accused, one should not pronounce him or her guilty, even if there is much popular clamor for conviction.

It is often difficult to arrive at a judgment on *circumstantial evidence*. Most crimes are committed in secret, so that direct evidence of the crime cannot be given. Sometimes, however, circumstantial evidence is as convincing as direct evidence. If a person, after a crime had been committed, should be seen burying a bloody weapon, and should thereafter be caught disposing of some articles taken from the body of a murdered man, the person's guilt would be presumed, if he or she could not give an entirely satisfactory explanation of these unusual acts. Though no one has seen the person committing the crime, this behavior shows that he or she is guilty. In all such matters the common sense, honesty, and character of the jury must be relied upon. This illustrates how our government rests upon the people, and how the people must stand back of every law if it is enforced.

The Punishment. — When the jury has returned its verdict, the judge pronounces judgment and determines the punishment of the crime under the law. It is then the privilege of the accused to make an appeal from the decision of the court to a higher tribunal, where the case will be definitely disposed of.

In the punishment of criminals two objects are sought, the protection of society and the reformation of the individual. In cases where the character of the criminal is such that any improvement is hopeless, — if, for instance, he or she has been inhuman enough to take the life of another person, — some commonwealths punish the criminal with death. In many states, however, imprisonment for life is the most severe punishment. We should, of course, consider that criminals are often unfortunate beings who have been driven to their desperate acts by unhappy conditions, but this should not lead us to weakness in dealing with them. They must be placed where they cannot do any further harm. Nevertheless, with all criminals, but especially with those guilty of less serious crimes, the effort should be made to inflict punishment in such a manner that their character may be improved and that they may be enabled to atone for their wrongdoing. Prisoners should be given an opportunity to do useful work, and every evidence of a desire to reform should be recognized and encouraged. When released from prison after their term of punishment has expired, they should be helped to obtain some honest occupation, that they may not be driven back to a criminal life.

Criminal laws deal with acts which are directed against the safety of all of us. When an individual is wounded, when a person's house is invaded by burglars, when thieves carry off the property of others, we all feel the danger to ourselves, and we demand that the government shall protect us against such acts and shall punish them as crimes against society itself.

Unjust Arrest. — The law also protects innocent persons against unjust arrest or imprisonment. When the liberty of any individual is restrained, the person's friends may go before any judge and get from him a writ of *habeas corpus* (Latin for "You may have the body"). This writ is a command of the court, directing the sheriff, or other person under whose control the prisoner may be, to bring said prisoner before the court and to show for what reason he or she is imprisoned. If no legal cause can be shown, the judge will then immediately set free the prisoner thus illegally restrained. In times of war the privilege of the writ of *habeas corpus* may be temporarily suspended. It is a great protection to the liberty of citizens against official tyranny or unjust persecution, that the legality of an arrest can thus at any time be tested.

QUESTIONS

1. Define feudal; acropolis; plaintiff; defendant; bail; extradite; venue; panel; *habeas corpus.*

2. What are some of the qualities that make a good police officer? A good judge?

3. How may crime be prevented?

4. What is the business of a juvenile court?

5. What is capital punishment? Is it justifiable?

6. What is "lynch law"?

7. How do you discriminate between a felony and a misdemeanor?

8. What are the duties of a sheriff? A constable?

9. Why were juvenile courts established? Have they helped any boys or girls to become better men and women? How?

10. Is a person guilty because arrested? What is "reasonable doubt"?

11. What is "circumstantial evidence"?

12. Why should criminals be punished?

CHAPTER VII

PROTECTION OF
THE CITIZENS

Protection of Property. — The government not only protects us against the acts of criminals, but it also protects our property and our health. One of the best-known departments of a city government is the fire department. Firefighters are paid by the city for watching over the property of citizens and protecting it against destruction by fire. If a fire alarm is given, they must immediately hasten with their apparatus to the scene of the fire and extinguish it. They are under the command of the chief of the department, who controls their action as a general does an army. In smaller places fire companies are made up of citizens who volunteer to do this service for the people. It is inspiring to see these brave and fearless firefighters at a great fire imperil their own lives to save lives and property of others.

Protection of Health. — Another service which the government performs is the protection of health. The Center for Disease Control focuses on infectious diseases. They are responsible for detecting and responding to new and emerging health threats, including birth defects, West Nile virus, Ebola, avian, swine, and pandemic flu, E. coli, and bioterrorism, to name a few. They also share information with public health care workers nationwide about chronic diseases, disabilities, injury control, workplace hazards, and environmental health threats.

U.S. Quarantine Stations are located at 20 ports of entry and land-border crossings where international travelers arrive. They are staffed with medical and public health officers who decide whether ill persons can enter the United States and what measures should be taken to prevent the spread of contagious diseases.

Health officers take many measures designed to protect the life and health of the public. All their requirements should be respected, for their observance, though inconvenient at the time, will protect us as well as others from much trouble and suffering.

Personal Rights. — Though an individual may not do direct violence to our person or destroy or injure our property, that person's actions may, nevertheless, be so injurious to us that we will not suffer them without complaint. Thus, one may refuse to fulfill one's promise, or to pay for goods bought from us; one may allow his cattle to pasture on our land; or one may tell falsehoods about us that injure our reputation. When such acts as these are not accompanied by direct violence or disorderly conduct, the state will not itself punish them by fine or imprisonment. They are not crimes against the state, but wrongs (or *torts*) against individuals. In such cases, the offender must make good whatever damage his act has caused. The state will assist its citizens in obtaining justice under such circumstances. The courts are open to any who wish to bring action against those who have infringed their legal rights. The duties that we owe our fellow-citizens and neighbors are not only recognized by our own sense of justice, but they are also defined and enforced by the laws of the state. These laws must be in accordance with the public conscience as to what is right and wrong. They ought not to forbid actions which are harmless in themselves simply because they are not pleasing to certain persons, nor ought they to allow acts to be committed by which any citizen will suffer injury.

Our Neighbors' Rights. — It is the law of the land that we must fulfill contracts which we have made. When we have promised to carry out a certain piece of work, or to rent lands or a house to another, or to sell an individual certain goods or to pay him or her a certain purchase price, we are bound in law to do as we have promised. We must also be considerate of the property rights, the health, and reputation of our fellow-citizens. We must not wantonly trespass upon their property, doing injury thereto. They have a right to forbid hunting or the picking of flowers upon their land. In fact, whenever we go upon the land of another person, we do it really without any right, and we should be careful not to do any injury to trees or fences or buildings. It is also wrong to do any act which injures the health of others, such as throwing refuse where it may become injurious. One's good name or reputation is one's most valuable possession. It is, therefore, a great wrong to accuse someone falsely of having done disreputable or criminal acts.

All such wrongful acts as these are called *torts*, and they may be punished by the courts. The person bringing the action is called the plaintiff. The one of whom the plaintiff complains is called the defendant. Both persons usually have attorneys, although in lower courts they will often state their own case without any such help. If either party desires it, the case will be tried before a jury. In a justice court the jury is composed of six jurors. In the higher courts it numbers twelve jurors, just like the jury in criminal cases. If the court decides for the plaintiff, it will condemn the defendant to the payment of a certain sum of money by way of damages. This money is not like a fine in a criminal court. A fine for criminal action goes to the state. In a civil action, however, the damages are paid to the plaintiff.

Action at Law to be Avoided. — A fair-minded citizen will not begin an action at law before attempting to settle the case outside of court. Most cases can be thus settled if both parties are reasonable. They will find a common meeting ground, a solution of the difficulty, which satisfies both. However, if one entirely disregards our rights and seems to wish to trample on them, it will be a great weakness on our part if we do not stand up for what is just. In such a case we are not only defending our own rights, but those of all other citizens. If we should weakly submit to wrong, the rights of others would also soon be attacked. It is only by defending our rights at all times against encroachment that we can secure and protect them. Sometimes we feel that it is less trouble to submit to injury, but it is always better to be firm in resisting wrong. Some time ago, when Mark Twain returned to New York City from Europe, a hack driver tried to exact from him four or five times the regular fare. The author was in haste, his time was valuable, and so the driver thought that it would be easy to impose upon him. But he had mistaken his man. The passenger insisted that the driver take him to the police headquarters. There he paid the rogue his regular fare, but made complaint of him for his exactions, and insisted upon his punishment for breaking the city ordinance. In speaking of this occurrence, Mark Twain said, "We can preserve great rights only by standing up for little rights." Where everybody is too busy to resist injustice, the time will come when justice will be forgotten, and personal rights will be ignored.

Imprisonment for Debt. — In former times, and not so very long ago, those who refused to pay their lawful debts were imprisoned. In our country we do not punish debtors in that way. We consider it better that such persons should be at liberty and be able to earn something in order that they may eventually pay their debts. However, should a person in obtaining money or goods from another person make entirely false statements of fact, that person is guilty of a crime, — that of obtaining money or goods under false pretences. For this wrong he or she may be imprisoned.

QUESTIONS

1. What would you do if someone arrested you without cause?

2. What is the meaning of an oath in a law court? What is the punishment of false witnesses?

3. What work does the clerk of the court do?

4. Should firefighters and police officers receive pensions?

5. Should people be forced to pay their just debts if they are able to do so? How can this be done?

6. Define *tort;* quarantine; insurance; bankrupt; contagious; compromise.

7. What is the difference between a civil and a criminal court?

8. What are the duties of a Board of Health? Why necessary?

CHAPTER VIII

EDUCATIONAL INSTITUTIONS

A Fundamental Principle. — In most modern states, and especially in our own, it is one of the principles upon which the state is founded that all the people should be trained sufficiently to do their own thinking and to be able to take a part in government as intelligent voters. A republican state must be founded upon the intelligence of its people. It is, therefore, essential that education should be open and free to all. It is because the state cannot do its work without intelligent citizens that it has itself undertaken the work of education. This work is supplemented by private schools, but in the main education in our country is free. Education tends to make all persons equal. If they have mental powers that fit them for great success in law or in some other profession, or if they have talents for invention or for engineering, these natural gifts are developed by the schools.

Public Schools. — The public school is a democratic institution. All kinds of children are here brought together. Their parents may be rich or poor, they may come from various backgrounds, — to the state they are all alike. Their opportunities are the same, and the same care is given to their education. Fine large, airy school buildings kept clean and neat within are provided for all. Attractive pictures make it a pleasure to be within their walls, a pleasure that will be long remembered. Teachers, trained in public or private institutions provided for that purpose, are in charge, and every facility is offered for a complete education.

The public schools are entirely under public control. The schools of a city or town are governed by a school board elected by the people or appointed by the mayor. This board makes regulations for the schools and administers their affairs. It makes contracts for new buildings; it selects teachers; it decides upon text-books; and it provides whatever may be needed for the efficient working of the schools. In fact, every interest connected with school work is controlled by this body. The excellence of the system of education in any town depends largely upon the intelligence and public spirit of the school board. The official director of the schools in the city or town is the superintendent.

Higher Education. — The higher branches of learning are taught in colleges and universities. Many of the great universities are private institutions, but nearly all the states have colleges and universities supported by the public. In these every variety of training adapted for the development of the varied talents of men and women is offered. In former times, universities existed apart from the life of the people. They devoted themselves to special refinement and to the study of difficult and recondite subjects. Today, however, especially in our own country, the university is a part of the life of the people. It interests itself in the general welfare of the state. It works to improve the agriculture, the manufacturing activities, the engineering work, the health, the power, of the commonwealth. It exists for every resident. If one has not the leisure to go to the university for a period to work there in person, one may receive instruction online, where his questions will be answered, and advice will be given. Lecturers are also sent by the university to various cities and towns of the state, where, in public discussions, they inform the people about things that are being done in their disciplines.

Land-Grant Institutions. — The Morrill Acts of 1862 and 1890 granted federal land to states, which they could sell to raise funds to establish and endow "land-grant" colleges. The amount of federal land a state received was in proportion to its population. As set forth in the 1862 Act, the mission of the land-grant institutions was to focus on the practical side of agriculture, science, and engineering. In 1887 federal funds were sent to states to establish a series of agricultural experiment stations under the direction of each state's land-grant college, with more funds given later to support cooperative extension — the sending of agents into rural areas to bring the results of agricultural research to farmers. Today each land-grant institution receives annual federal appropriations for research and extension work on the condition that those funds are matched by state funds.

Inventions. — The American nation is noted for its talent for invention. We readily recall many notable inventions that were made in this country. We need only think of the steam-engine, the telephone, the electric light bulb, and the PC. This talent for invention is perhaps due to the fact that our nation found itself in a new and extensive territory, under novel conditions which brought out the power to adapt our action to our needs and to fit ourselves with new means of supplying them. This talent is cultivated by institutions of learning. While they cannot endow an individual with genius, they can give him or her the materials to work with. They can teach what other people have already achieved and along what lines new enterprises will be most promising.

Public Libraries. — Another great educational influence in our country comes from public libraries. Nearly every town now has an institution of this kind. There we can get stories and books of travel to provide entertainment for long winter evenings. We can also find books which will inform us about the history of our own and of other nations, about our political institutions, about the facts of science, and about many other important and useful matters. In every home there should be a library of the books that are dearest and most useful to the members of the family, but we can none of us own all the books we need. The public library enables us to get at any time the information required for our purpose. Very often entertaining and useful lectures are given at the library. It is an excellent place to spend a leisure hour, because while being most agreeably entertained we are also improving our minds and increasing our knowledge.

Mr. Carnegie, a man who lacked the advantages of an education in his early youth, but who later became very successful and immensely rich, has given a large number of libraries to our country. He has said that it was his purpose that other people should be able to have the advantages which he lacked. He believed most thoroughly in the importance of general education for the welfare of our country. Such public gifts are laudable, but it would be unfortunate if the people of this country were to rely entirely on gifts of this nature. That has greatest value which costs us time and labor and self-denial. If some generous person has provided our town with a library building, we should make use of the opportunity and give liberal support to the library itself, in order that it may make the life of our neighborhood better in every way.

Many public libraries today offer access to computers connected to the internet.

It is one of the most beneficent features of modern civilization that the best things in life, and the most interesting, can be brought to us wherever we live. It is not necessary that we live in New York or Chicago in order to get the latest news every morning, or to be able to read the great works of literature, or to hear fine music and see beautiful pictures. All these things are brought to us, even in the remotest parts of our country, through the inventions by which distance has been annihilated and the reproduction of works of art has been made possible. So the library in every town ought to be the center of interest in the wonderful achievements which it is our privilege to enjoy. How unfortunate the community which lives only for itself, and does not share in the enjoyment of art, literature, music, and all the gracious influences that this marvelous age provides!

QUESTIONS

1. How large is the income of the public library in your town, and how is it funded?

2. Is your school board elected or appointed? Name its members.

3. What rules are there for homeschoolers in your state?

4. Should school books be furnished without cost to pupils? Why, or why not?

5. Is free education beyond the high school available in your state? Ought it to be?

6. How much money is expended annually to support the schools of your city or town?

7. What does it cost in your city or town to school one pupil for a year?

8. Name some modern-day inventions Americans were responsible for.

9. What land-grant institutions are there in your state?

CHAPTER IX

HEALTH AND SAFETY

The health of all our residents depends on the quality of the air we breathe, the water we drink, and the food we are eat.

Air Quality. — Air quality is compromised by a number of sources. Wildfires, lightning strikes, volcanic eruptions, and dust storms are natural occurrences that contribute to air pollution. Other sources of pollution are man-made. Mobile sources, including automobiles, buses, trucks, airplanes, and trains, account for more than half of all the air pollution in the United States, with automobiles powered by fossil fuels being the major contributor. Stationary sources, such as power plants, oil refineries, industrial facilities, and factories, emit large amounts of pollution from a single location. These are also called point sources of pollution since they emanate from a single place. The last major source of pollution comes from areas of high population, namely cities, and areas high in agricultural activity, especially livestock operations.

Types of Air Pollution. — Ozone, particulates, carbon monoxide, sulfur dioxide, and nitrogen oxides are the principal types of air pollution in the United States today.

Ozone. — Ozone is not emitted but is formed through a chemical reaction between sunlight and gases such as carbon monoxide and nitrogen oxides that are emitted by the burning of fossil fuels. This ground level ozone pollution is generally highest during the sunniest months of the year, from May through October.

Particle Pollution. — Particle pollution is a mixture of solids and liquid droplets floating in the air. Some particles are released directly from a specific source, while others form through complex chemical reactions that occur in the atmosphere. Particles vary greatly in size. Small particles, 10 micrometers or less in diameter, are small enough that they can enter the lungs, potentially causing serious health problems. Fine particles (2.5 micrometers or smaller) are produced by all types of combustion including that in motor vehicles and power plants, as well as by forest fires, residential wood burning, and agricultural burning. Coarse dust particles (2.5 to 10 micrometers) come from crushing or grinding operations, dust stirred up by vehicles on roads, and windstorms.

Carbon Monoxide. — Carbon monoxide is produced by the incomplete burning of fossil fuels in motor vehicles, industrial plants, and home heating equipment. A colorless and odorless gas, carbon monoxide is poisonous to animals and people when it is inhaled.

Sulfur Dioxide. — Sulfur dioxide is produced by

the burning of fuels that contain sulfur, including oil and coal. In the atmosphere it combines with water droplets to form sulfuric acid, a major component of acid rain that has destroyed vast areas of forest, and made many lakes and streams too acidic to support fish and other aquatic life.

Nitrogen Oxides. — Nitrogen oxides are produced during the combustion of fuels at high temperatures, such as occurs in the engines of motor vehicles and ships. Nitrogen oxides are also produced naturally by lightning. Nitrogen oxides contribute to both smog and acid rain.

Reduction in Air Pollution. — Due to concerted efforts in recent decades to curb air pollution through a series of Clean Air Acts, air pollution has dropped dramatically since 1970. Carbon monoxide and sulfur dioxide emissions have fallen by half, nitrogen oxide emissions by one-third, particulate emissions by 80% and lead emissions by more than 98%. Because air pollution has so many adverse effects on the health of children and those suffering from respiratory and cardiovascular diseases, however, further reduction is warranted.

Monitoring Air Pollution. — Since air naturally moves, air pollution moves too. Air movement is affected by wind direction, wind velocity, temperature variations, and terrain. So air pollution in a given area may vary from one day to the next and even from one hour to the next. The Environmental Protection Agency collects data from air quality monitors throughout the country, computes the Air Quality Index for each area, and publishes maps and charts on its airnow.gov website. On these maps, each of the six severity levels — 0-50 (Healthy), 51-100 (Moderate), 101-150 (Unhealthy for sensitive groups), 151-200 (Unhealthy), 201-300 (Very unhealthy), 301-500 (Hazardous) — is coded in a different color, with orange, red, purple, and maroon indicating increasing hazard. Local news outlets typically inform the public if local air quality is code orange or above, so sensitive individuals can limit outdoor exposure as necessary. At the airnow.gov website, you can view current and forecasted Air Quality Index for any state or zipcode.

Water Supply. — The water we drink is as necessary to life as the air we breathe. We can get water from either surface water or groundwater. Surface water is the water we see in lakes, streams, rivers, and oceans. It is replenished by rain (or other precipitation) and by water flowing from tributaries upstream. Groundwater is stored underground in aquifers, porous layers of rock, sand, and gravel through which water can move. Groundwater is replenished in early spring by rain and snowmelt and at other times of heavy precipitation so long as the ground is not frozen. Much of the water in aquifers may have been deposited there years ago.

Water in aquifers is accessed by drilling a well. Over 15% of the U.S. population depends on private wells for their water supply. Another 27% relies on groundwater supplied by public water systems. Most of the U.S. population, though, including millions of people in large metropolitan areas, count on surface water for their supply. New York City, for example, derives its water from three different watersheds, which feed more than a dozen reservoirs and controlled lakes, to serve over a billion gallons a day to its 9 million customers.

The New York City water is so pure that it only needs to be disinfected before delivered to residents, but surface water in most other localities requires a more complex water treatment before it is fit for human consumption. The Environmental Protection Agency, charged with issuing federal regulations for public water systems by the Safe Drinking Water Act of 1974, sets standards for water quality. States and other local governments are responsible for enforcing the standards.

Water Pollution. — Water pollution is the build up of one or more substances in water to the point that the water containing them becomes harmful to people and animals. Pollution is typically measured in parts per million. Most toxic substances are not harmful at very low levels, but become so when a large amount is deposited in a small amount of water. The large amount can be released all at once from a single source, or in small amounts over a longer period of time from multiple sources. You can observe how pollutants might be diluted by pouring a small amount of food dye into a small amount of water, then notice how the food dye becomes less and less visible as you add more and more water.

Two especially potent sources of water pollution are sewage and chemical fertilizers used in agriculture that make their way into rivers. Both of these sources of nutrients can spur a great increase in the growth of algae or plankton that spreads broadly in rivers, lakes, and oceans. This harmful algal bloom, by removing oxygen from the water, can kill many forms of life, resulting in what is called a dead zone. In a recent summer, one such zone in the Gulf of Mexico grew to over 8,000 square miles, an area the size of New Jersey.

Waste water is another significant source of pollution. It includes industrial waste discharged by factories, as well as detergents used in homes, weed killers used in gardens, and petroleum products washed off roads by heavy rain events.

Among the most toxic of wastes are PCBs, once used in the manufacture of electronic circuit boards, heavy metals (lead, cadmium, and mercury), and radioactive waste.

Last, but not least, is oil pollution. The most visible oil spill in recent memory is the BP oil spill in the Gulf of Mexico in 2012 which spewed an estimated 4.9 million barrels of oil into the Gulf, causing massive die-off of wildlife and extensive damage to marine habitat.

Both surface water and groundwater are affected by water pollution, but pollution of groundwater in certain locations may be irreversible because of geological formations limiting water flow. Surface water (excepting oceans and lakes with no outlets) always flows downstream, carrying its pollutants with it. Surface water is recharged by falling rain and water flowing from upstream tributaries, so as water pollution decreases in upstream tributaries, the amount of pollution in streams, rivers, and lakes will decrease as well. The oceans, however, are a different story. Since they have no outlet, everything that flows into them remains within their waters. As a result, the oceans of the world are becoming increasingly polluted.

The Environmental Protection Agency is responsible for monitoring water pollution within our borders and issuing regulations to control it, but global collaboration will be required to clean up pollution in the oceans.

Residential Water Use. — Americans use an average of 80 to 100 gallons per person per day, Europeans half as much. Indoor water use is decreasing though with the advent of water-saving dishwashers and washing machines, as well as low flow faucets, shower heads, and toilets. In times of drought state and local governments often impose restrictions on water use, especially on outdoor activities such as watering the lawn or washing cars.

Agricultural Water Use. — While residential water use accounts for only 6% of U.S. water consumption, agricultural use for irrigation amounts to 81% of water used. Many farmers are trying to decrease their use of water through a variety of techniques:

1. Reduction of water run-off by planting on contour and growing of cover crops.

2. Capturing and storing water in ponds and swales.

3. Increasing water-holding capacity of soil by

adding compost, growing cover crops, using no-till techniques, and practicing rotational grazing.

4. Irrigating more efficiently by using drip lines to deposit water where it is needed and scheduling irrigation at times when it is most needed.

Floods. — However carefully farmers manage the water on their farms, there will always be heavy rain events that cause flooding. These may be locally heavy thunderstorms that cause flooding in a limited area or Category 5 hurricanes that cause flooding over an extensive region. Rapid snowmelt results in rising streams that may cause rivers downstream to overflow their banks.

Federal Emergency Management Agency. — Widespread devastation caused by flooding is a civil emergency. If the flooding is a disaster that overwhelms the resources of state and local authoritites, the governor of the state where the flooding occurs can declare a state of emergency and ask the President to order the Federal Emergency Management Agency (FEMA) and the federal government to respond to the disaster. As an agency of the Department of Homeland Security, FEMA's primary purpose is to coordinate the response to disasters. In conjunction with volunteer organizations such as the Red Cross, FEMA helps set up care centers as soon as possible to provide for the immediate needs of the victims for water, food, shelter, and medical care. Then FEMA assists with long term needs, such as housing, debris removal, and rebuilding of infrastructure. FEMA also coordinates the response to other types of disasters, including tornadoes, earthquakes, and spills of hazardous substances.

Food Safety. — The responsibility for ensuring the safety of our food is shared between the federal government and the states. Two agencies of the federal government provide principal oversight. The United State Department of Agriculture (USDA) is responsible for the safety of meat, poultry, and processed egg products, while the Food and Drug Administration (FDA) bears responsibility for the safety of other types of food. Some states have their own food safety programs for handling food-borne diseases or monitoring levels of pesticide in produce.

QUESTIONS

1. What are some ways to decrease air pollution?

2. How are the members of your family likely to be affected by air pollution?

3. Look up the Air Quality Index for your state and your zipcode. What category does it fall into?

4. Name four sources of water pollution.

5. How can farmers minimize agricultural run-off from their farms?

CHAPTER X

TRANSPORTATION

Early History. — The growth of the United States is closely tied to advances in transportation technology. The early settlers arrived in sailing ships and made their homes along the coast by natural harbors or navigable waterways. Transportation over land in those days was by horse and buggy and along the coast by sailing ship. Early attempts at road-building resulted in roads that were often muddy and impassable at certain times of the year, but gradually a small network of roads was developed to connect the coastal cities and smaller settlements inland.

The completion of the Erie Canal in 1825 connected Lake Erie with the Hudson River through 83 separate locks and over a distance of 363 miles. Goods could now be shipped by water all the way from New York City, up the Hudson River to the Erie Canal, along the Erie Canal to Buffalo on Lake Erie, and from there to all points west on the Great Lakes. Similarly, goods from Duluth on the western edge of Lake Superior could be transported to Chicago, Detroit, Cleveland, and Buffalo, and via the Erie Canal, even to the Eastern

Seaboard. Commerce and settlement exploded in the upper midwest as a result.

The invention of the steamboat in the early 1800s accelerated that development, especially in the midwest and south. Not only was the steamboat used on Lake Ontario and the other Great Lakes, but it made the Mississippi River, and its two major tributaries, the Ohio and the Missouri, navigable in both directions.

As railroads expanded in the period before the Civil War, the importance of natural waterways and canals diminished. Railroads offered a way to transport goods and people year-round, both reliably and quickly. With the industrialization that occurred after the Civil War and the building of the Transcontinental Railroad, railroads spread quickly to connect industries and growing population centers on both coasts and the great expanse of land in between.

Roads and Highways. — The debut in 1908 of the Model T Ford, an automobile which was both mass-produced and affordable for many Americans, led to the demise of the railroad as the predominant form of transportation for people, and ushered in a renewed focus on the building of roads. Rural voters asked for paved roads with the slogan "Get the farmers out of the mud!"

With the Federal Highway Act of 1921 funding was made available to state highway departments to build two-lane paved interstate highways. Depression-era job-creation programs provided the labor for many such projects. Finally, in 1956 President Dwight David

Eisenhower signed the Federal Aid Highway Act, laying the foundation for the controlled-access interstate highway system we have today. The original portion of the interstate highway system was completed in 1991, serving nearly all major U.S. cities. This high-speed, high-capacity network has since been extended and, as of 2013, it had a total length of 47,856 miles criss-crossing the country. Today, about one-quarter of all vehicle miles driven in the United States use the interstate system, an impressive percentage considering that there are over 3.9 million miles of highway in the U.S. People today do most of their traveling by automobile, both for long-distance trips and daily commutes. In fact 87% of passenger-miles traveled occurs in cars, trucks, vans, and motorcycles. Of all the countries in the world, U.S. residents have the highest rate of vehicle ownership, with 865 vehicles for each 1000 residents.

Air Travel. — Though there was some passenger air travel in the 1920s and 1930s, it wasn't until after World War II that passenger air travel surged. It became the preferred method of traveling the long distance from one coast to the other and between major cities that were far apart. As confidence in the safety of airplanes increased, so did the number of passengers. Today passenger air travel accounts for 12% of passenger-miles, with 719 million passengers on domestic flights in 2016 alone. The U.S. has extensive infrastructure to support air travel, with 86 airports handling over one million passengers a year. Though the airlines are privately owned companies, security for air travel is handled by the Transportation Security Administration (TSA), an agency of the Department of Homeland Security. Every passenger must show a valid federal or state ID and submit to a scan or search to make sure they have no prohibited items before boarding an airplane.

Railroads. — Until the middle of the 20th century, traveling by train was the predominant mode of passenger travel. But the building of the Interstate Highway System and the rise in air travel after World War II delivered a one-two punch to train travel from which the rail system has never recovered. Today Amtrak provides the only passenger rail system between cities in the continental U.S. It operates over 22,000 miles of track, but doesn't own any of it. Instead Amtrak pays fees to freight railroads for using theirs. More than a dozen metropolitans areas have commuter rail systems, but since there are few connections between them, long distance travel on commuter rail systems is all but impossible. Fewer than 1% of passenger miles are traveled by rail.

Bicycles. — Commuting to work is growing in the U.S. In Portland, Oregon 7% of commuters cycle to work, while in Madison, Wisconsin and Minneapolis, Minnesota, 5% do. In Copenhagen, Denmark, on the other hand, fully 50% of the population commutes by bike to work or school. Citizens of Copenhagen log twice as many kilometers by bike as they do by Metro.

Waterways. — A very small number of passenger-miles are traveled by water. Passengers on ferries crossing rivers or ferries between islands and the mainland account for most of the passenger miles by water.

Cargo. — For cargo, though, it is a different story, with 7% of ton-miles of freight conveyed over water. Railroads, too, play a significant role in movement of goods, with 26% of ton-miles of goods traveling by rail. Trucks carry the largest amount of freight, accounting for 43% of ton-miles of freight. Pipelines, in conveying oil and natural gas, transport 15% of ton-miles of freight. Airplanes, which carry only the most perishable and time-critical freight, account for less than 1% of the ton-miles of freight. Some freight, amounting to 9%, is carried by two or more different ways, partially by truck and partially by train for example, or partially by barge and partially by train.

Mass Transit. — Mass transit is not as popular in the United States as it is in many other countries, primarily due to suburban sprawl. The closer together people live, the more likely they are to use mass transit. Most medium-sized cities have some form of public transportation, typically a network of bus routes. Larger cities frequently have light-rail systems for moving lots of passengers within the urban setting, and commuter rail to transport riders from the suburbs. One-third of the nation's mass transit riders live in New York City, where they are served by buses and rail, as well as the subway. While the New York City mass transit system serves 9 million riders a week, the Moscow mass transit systems serves 7 million a day. To put it another way, Moscow has more than 5 times the number of riders that New York City has, even though its population is only 1½ times as large.

QUESTIONS

1. How do you think the repair of crumbling bridges should be funded?

2. Do you think the U.S. government should subsidize the passenger rail system? Why or why not?

3. What are the benefits of mass transit?

4. Do you think the U.S. government should subsidize mass transit? Why or why not?

5. Owners of gasoline-powered cars support the maintenance of roads through the gasoline taxes they pay. Should owners of electric cars also subsidize the maintenance of roads, and if so, how?

6. How do you think the advent of self-driving vehicles will change the face of transportation in the United States?

CHAPTER XI

WATERWAYS

Inland Waterways. — There are more than 25,000 miles of navigable waterways within the interior of the United States. Most of these are in the eastern half of the country. Only the Columbia River on the West Coast is navigable for any distance. Rapid changes in elevation and irregular water flow make western rivers ideal for hydroelectric projects, but not for navigation.

The Mississippi River, with its major tributaries, the Ohio and the Missouri, along with the Hudson, and the Great Lakes, are some of the more important waterways in the East. With the Illinois Waterway connecting the Great Lakes to the Mississippi River, shipments can travel from the St. Lawrence Seaway to the Gulf of Mexico. It is the job of the Army Corps of Engineers to dredge the 12,000 miles of inland waterways as needed to allow for navigation. The Corps also operates 235 locks, to move barges from one elevation to another. Through these waterways pass about 16% of the nation's inland freight, including coal, petroleum, corn, and soybeans, at a cost much cheaper than by rail or truck.

Harbors. — The Army Corps of Engineers also

maintains our harbors and constructs our harbor works. Whether the harbor is on a river, like New Orleans, or a lake, like Milwaukee, or on the ocean, like San Diego, the cost of improvements, dredging and marking the channels, building breakwaters, piers, and jetties, is borne by the nation as a whole.

Lighthouses. — A lighthouse is a tower, building, or other type of structure designed to emit light from a system of lamps and lenses, and to serve as a navigational aid for maritime pilots at sea or on inland waterways. Historically, every headland, the entrance to every harbor, every prominent or dangerous point on the Great Lakes, had its light to warn and guide the mariner. At one time there were more than 3300 lighthouses and lighted aids to navigation in this country, 1800 being post lights used chiefly on rivers. But the number of operational lighthouses has declined drastically in recent years due to the expense of maintaining them and the rapid increase in use of electronic navigational systems.

QUESTIONS

1. Mention some of the principal waterways of the United States.

2. What purpose does the Illinois Waterway serve?

3. Why do waterways and harbors need to be dredged?

4. What is the use of a lock in a canal?

CHAPTER XII

PUBLIC UTILITIES

City versus Country. — If we lived in the country, we would likely depend upon wells for water for domestic uses. For heat we might burn kerosene, or even wood. In cities, however, these services are provided to us for a fee. Our water is supplied from distant reservoirs and brought through pipes to our houses. Gas or electricity from some public source of supply furnishes us with heat.

Infrastructure. — Consider all the infrastructure that is involved in delivering water to customers. Reservoirs may have to be constructed to store water, one or more water treatment plants must be built to treat water, a network of pipes must be laid underground to deliver water to customers, and another network of larger pipes to collect the sewage and transport it to a sewage treatment plant. Different infrastructure will be needed to supply electricity, natural gas, telephone, and broadband services.

Public Utilities. — Public utilities are organizations that take on the task of building and maintaining infrastructure so they can provide services to consumers.

Some of the consumers of services are residential, but others are commercial or industrial. Because the infrastructure needed to deliver water, electricity, natural gas, and other services is so expensive to build and maintain, it doesn't make sense for a second company to build a competing infrastructure, if another company has already done it. So, usually, the first company that builds out the infrastructure has a monopoly.

The monopoly will be a government monopoly if it is publicly owned. Publicly-owned utilities are non-profit. They may be cooperative utilities that are owned by the customers they serve or they may be municipal utilities owned by a branch of local government.

Public utilities, so-called because they serve the public, can also be privately owned. These investor-owned utilities are owned by investors and are operated for a profit.

Public Utilities Commissions. — Every state has a commission that regulates the rates and services of public utilities within that state. These commissions go by different names, with some being called Public Service Commission and others called Public Utilities Commission, or a variation thereof. These commissions are responsible for seeing to it that public utilities provide an appropriate level of service for a reasonable rate. As costs and service requirements rise, public utilities typically apply for rate increases to cover the increased expense. These commissions evaluate the requests for rate increases to make sure they are justified before approving them.

QUESTIONS

1. Make a list of all the utilities that service your home.

2. Where does the drinking water in your house come from? What is its cost per month?

3. How is the electricity for your house generated? What is its cost per month? Is the cost the same from one month to the next or does it vary depending on the season?

4. What percentage of electricity in your state is generated by a renewable resource such as hydroelectric power, wind turbines, or solar panels?

5. Does your state have a plan for increasing the percentage of electricity generated by renewable resources?

6. Which of your utilities are publicly owned and which are privately owned?

7. Some localities are offering broadband services at no cost to their residents. Do you think all localities should?

CHAPTER XIII

FORESTS

The Forest Primeval. — The territory of the land that became the United States was originally covered with vast forests. It is estimated that in 1630 that 46% of the total land area was forested, amounting to 1,023 million acres. When the European settlers arrived on the Eastern seaboard, many valuable kinds of timber abounded, — pine, fir, hemlock, oak, and others. They immediately began cutting timber to clear land for farming the way their ancestors had done, not realizing that the Native Americans had different agricultural practices that served them well. They created small fields using slash and burn techniques and planted in mounds within the openings. As fields decreased in fertility, they moved their agricultural efforts to new fields which they created the same way, allowing the old fields to return to a forested state.

Clearing of the Land. — After the arrival of the settlers, about 256 million acres of forest land were cleared or burned to prepare it for the growing of agricultural crops. Clearing proceeded steadily from 1630 onward, but accelerated rapidly in the second half of the 19th century when an estimated 13 square miles of forest were cleared every day for 50 years. Since the early 1900s the amount of forest land has remained relatively steady at about 760 million acres, even as the population of the United States has tripled.

United States Forest Service — Alarmed by the rapid destruction of the forests, successive presidents of the United States, Mr. Cleveland, Mr. McKinley, and Mr. Roosevelt, took up the cause of forest preservation around the turn of the 20th century, and urged legislation upon Congress by which our forests would be protected. Their efforts resulted in the establishment of the United States Forest Service in 1905. Today the Forest Service manages 155 national forests and 20 grasslands, comprising 193 million acres — an area larger that the states of South Carolina and Texas combined.

The Forest Service has as its mission "to sustain the health, diversity, and productivity of the nation's forests and grasslands to meet the needs of present and future generations." In other words, the Forest Service has to balance competing objectives. It has to protect resources and provide land for recreation, while also opening land for grazing, cutting of timber, and other resource extraction.

State Forests. — Thirty-eight of the states have also created forest reserves upon land belonging to them in order to preserve choice forest areas. They are managed in much the same way as the national forests, although, of course, they are much smaller.

Distribution of Forests. — The forests of the United States are very diverse, with all regions except the Great Plains having a heavy forest cover. Oak-hickory and maple-beech-birch forests dominate in the North, with extensive pine forests in the South. The Great Smoky Mountains in the southern Appalachians are home to more tree species than in all of Europe. Majestic Douglas-fir and ponderosa pines tower in the West.

Fire Management. — For many years fire in our nation's forests was suppressed at all costs. But with the realization that many forest ecosystems depend upon periodic fires to regenerate themselves, the fire management strategy has shifted. Low intensity fires started naturally are now allowed to burn where they are no threat to property or the public. This eliminates the accumulation of high fuel levels that can result in high intensity fires that decimate forests from top to bottom.

Carbon Sequestration. — The United States has the fourth largest forest area, after Russia, Brazil, and Canada. So our forests serve as one of the most important carbon sinks on earth.

Water Retention. — Forests play a critical role in regulating the flow of water. The leafy tree tops slow the fall of rain to the ground, where it is absorbed by organic matter on the forest floor, which acts a bit like a gigantic sponge. Depending upon the composition of the soil, the forest floor can absorb an enormous amount of rain, up to 18 inches. It then releases the water gradually to flow into streams or recharge the water table, with the result that areas downstream can have water even in times of drought.

Flood Control. — By absorbing water quickly and releasing it slowly, forests help prevent floods during heavy rainfall events.

Pollutant Removal. — Forests also play a critical role in filtering water that runs off from impervious surfaces and agricultural areas. Trees are very efficient in removing pollutants such as nitrates and phosphates, as well as heavy metals and petroleum products from soil and water.

Forest Products. — In addition to timber harvests for sawlogs, veneer logs, and pulpwood, the forest provides other products for human use. This includes herbal medicines, resins and oils for aromatics, raw materials for arts and crafts, furs for clothing, and food. Foraging for wild plant foods is a hobby for a small portion of our population, but hunting for deer, moose, and other big game animals, as well as migratory game birds, such as ducks and geese, is a time-honored tradition in our country.

QUESTIONS

1. Have you ever been to a national forest or grassland? Are there any in your state?

2. Does your state have any state forests? If so, locate the one nearest to you.

3. How has the management of forest fires changed over the years?

4. What benefits do forests provide?

CHAPTER XIV

PARKS

National Parks. — The United States has 59 national parks located in 27 states, totaling over 52.2 million acres, or an area about the size of Kansas. The national parks preserve some of the most spectacular scenery in the country, including that at Yellowstone National Park and Yosemite National Park, both famous the world over. While some national parks have been have been chosen for their natural beauty or unique geological features, others were selected because they represent unusual ecosystems or provide phenomenal recreational opportunities. The most-visited national park is Great Smoky Mountains National Park straddling the border between North Carolina and Tennessee, which boasts over 11 million visitors a year. The Grand Canyon National Park in Arizona comes in second with almost 6 million visitors.

National Monuments. — 129 areas in the United States have been declared national monuments either by presidential proclamation or by act of Congress. The Antiquities Act of 1906 gave the President the authority to name "historic landmarks, historic and prehistoric structures, and other objects of historic or scientific interest" as national monuments. Many of the monuments have a historical significance, with 23 containing artifacts and remnants of dwellings of Native Americans of an earlier era. Twelve forts are counted among the 33 other historical sites. Geological sites, marine sites, and volcanic sites are a few of the 65 monuments selected for their natural significance. Arizona leads the states with 18 national monuments within its borders. Following it are California with 17, and New Mexico with 14.

National Wildlife Refuges. — National Wildlife Refuges have as their goal the conservation of America's fish, wildlife and plants. Managed by the U.S. Fish and Wildlife Service, the National Wildlife Refuge System encompasses over 150 million acres in 562 national wildlife refuges and 38 wetland management districts. Every state has at least one refuge. In areas where recreational use is compatible with conservation efforts, opportunities for hunting, fishing, birding, photography, and environmental education are made available to the public. Refuges welcome nearly 50 million visitors annually. The National Wildlife Refuge System faces challenges on many sides, including habitat fragmentation, degradation of water quantity and quality, changes in climate, and invasive species, as well as increasing demands for recreation and development.

State Parks. — Over 10,000 state parks provide places of natural beauty, historic significance, and recreational opportunity close to home for most U.S.

residents. Most of the nearly 800 million annual visitors take day trips to state parks, but those who want overnight accommodations can select from over 160 lodges, 9,400 cabins and cottages, and 240,000 campsites. For the hiker there are over 9,000 hiking trails extending over 38,000 miles, including short trails that can be easily traversed and longer trails that are more challenging. Some of the parks maintained by states include Itasca State Park, with over 100 lakes at the head waters of the Mississippi River in the state of Minnesota, Niagara Falls State Park in New York, overlooking one of nature's wonders, and the Adirondack Park in the same state, amidst the delightful mountain scenery adjoining Lake Champlain. State parks have lots of benefits. They not only help to preserve natural ecosystems, while providing recreational opportunities of various sorts, they also offer open space in natural settings for those who might not otherwise have access to it and increase appreciation of our natural resources among those who visit.

City Parks. — Parks are to a city what a flower-garden is to a home. They do not bring any income, but in the enjoyment which the people get from them they pay many times over for any outlay of money which they may require. Some of our large cities have very extensive park systems. Central Park in New York City, Lincoln Park in Chicago, and Fairmount Park in Philadelphia, are extensive grounds beautified by trees, shrubs, and flowers, with lakes, waterfalls, and fountains to furnish variety, and collections of wild animals to lend interest.

QUESTIONS

1. Name four national parks and their distinguishing features. Are there any in your state?

2. How many state parks does your state have? Which are closest to you?

3. What national wildlife refuges are in your region of the country? What kinds of wildlife do they support?

CHAPTER XV

MONEY

The Medium of Exchange. — Money is one of the most necessary instruments of modern civilization. We all know how necessary it is to our own personal convenience. If there were no money, all exchanges would have to be made directly. If we had manufactured some chairs, but needed a horse, we should have to hunt about for a man who was in need of chairs and desired to dispose of a horse. Money enables us to save all this trouble. The person who wants our chairs comes to us and pays us in cash, which we can take and exchange for anything we desire. It is, however, very important that this money should be the same the country over, and that it should be perfectly safe and stable in its value. If a dollar should be worth one hundred cents today and only seventy-five cents next month, great loss and uncertainty would result in business affairs.

The National Currency. — The government undertakes to give us a stable national currency. The national government has the sole right to coin money and to issue paper currency. Even if one took the pure silver and stamped upon it the same symbols that are seen on our dollar, this action would be against the law and would be punished. No one is permitted to issue money except the federal government. The money issued is either of metal or of paper. The National Mint is responsible for coinage. In the early days of the National Mint, coins were minted using almost pure copper, silver, and gold. Today it issues copper-and-zinc cents, and copper-and-nickel five-cent pieces, dimes, half-dollars, and dollars. The Mint also produces commemorative gold and silver bullion coins.

A Substitute for Coin. — Paper money is also issued by the government, specifically by the Bureau of Engraving and Printing. The Bureau is responsible for both the design and printing of the paper notes, and at times updates or redesigns bills to improve their security and prevent counterfeiting. We should be able to get gold or silver at any time in return for the paper issued by the government. If the government should issue too much paper money, it would fall in value and cause great confusion and loss. No matter how rich a government is, its credit is limited, like that of an individual. In other words, there is a limit beyond which people will not lend it any money.

QUESTIONS

1. Why does the government issue a national currency? What were the circumstances that led to ours?

2. What gives a coin its value?

3. What gives a ten-dollar bill its value?

4. What is counterfeiting? Why ought it to be punished?

5. Why cannot state or local governments coin money?

6. Describe the designs on United States coins and bills. What do you think they mean?

7. Research the coins and bills of another country. What do they tell you about that country? How are they similar to and different from ours?

8. What means are taken to prevent the counterfeiting of our currency?

10. What is a mint? Where are the United States mints located?

11. Do all peoples use money as a medium of exchange? Why not? What are some other practices?

12. Why are some coins worth more than their face value? Name two.

CHAPTER XVI

COMMUNICATION

United States Postal Service. — One of the most important branches of the federal government is the United State Postal Service. Centuries ago, if one desired to send a letter to a person at a distance, one would have to employ a special messenger for the purpose. Later, the service of carrying letters for the public was conducted by private enterprise. By the time our government was founded, other governments had established a mail service, so that this became one of the lines of work undertaken by the United States from the very beginning. It is a great convenience to be able to drop a letter into a near-by mail-box, and without further care, and at a minimal expense, to have it delivered safely and quickly to a location in the most distant part of the country. The U.S. Postal Service is legally obligated to serve all residents of the United States and its territories at the same price and with the same level of service. A First-Class postage stamp costs the same whether you are mailing a letter to an address down the street or in the furthest reaches of Alaska.

The U.S. Postal Service delivers more mail to more

addresses in a larger geographical area than any other postal service in the world. In doing so, it handles 47% of the world's mail. In a recent year it delivered over 150 billion pieces of mail to over 150 million addresses in every town, village, and city in the country. With over 600,000 employees, it staffs more than 31,000 post offices and operates over 200,000 vehicles, comprising one of the largest civilian fleets in the world.

Classes of Mail. — Mail is divided into several classes. *First-Class* mail is for letters and small packages. The rate for First-Class mail varies by size and weight but not by distance. Items sent by First-Class mail are typically delivered within 2 to 3 days.

There are five different classes of mail for packages, which differ based on speed of delivery and restrictions on package contents. In order from most expensive to least expensive, these are:

Priority Mail Express (formerly called Express Mail) offering overnight delivery to most locations, with tracking included. Price varies by weight and distance.

Priority Mail delivering packages within one to three days, depending on the distance between origin and destination of shipment. Price varies by weight, size, and distance. Tracking is included.

USPS Retail Ground (formerly called Parcel Post) transporting all packages by ground or sea. Expected delivery time is 2 to 9 days between locations in the contiguous U.S., 4 to 14 days to Alaska and Hawaii, and 3 to 6 weeks to outlying areas. Rates vary by weight, size, and distance.

Media Mail (formerly called Book Rate) offering shipping for books and recorded media only. Rates vary based on weight, but not size or distance. Delivery times are similar to that of *USPS Retail Ground,* but rates are considerably cheaper.

Library Mail offering shipping for books and recorded media only. Similar to Media Mail, it is cheaper, but can only be used by public libraries, academic institutions, and museums.

Discounts are available for large volumes of mail through the *Bulk Mail* program. Additional requirements apply.

Other Services. — Post offices also provide other services including money-orders, certified mail, registered mail, and passports.

Money-orders provide a way for a person without a bank account to transmit money to a person or business in another location. The person purchasing a money order at the post office pays the full amount up front in cash, plus a small fee. Then the purchaser fills in his or her name and contact information on the front of the money order, along with the name and contact information of the recipient.

Certified Mail provides the sender with proof of mailing and a record of its delivery. It is often used for mailing legal documents.

Registered Mail provides the sender with a secure way of sending valuable or irreplaceable items.

Registered mail is transported in locked containers, separate from other mail. Tracking is included and insurance is available.

Passports are required to enter foreign countries and to re-enter the United States upon return. A person wanting a passport files an application in person at a post office.

Competition. — The U.S. Postal Service has exclusive access to letter boxes marked "U.S. Mail" and to the private letterboxes or mailboxes of individuals and businesses, giving them a monopoly on First-Class mail. Not so for package delivery though. Competitors such as FedEx and United Parcel Service have sprung up to provide alternatives to package delivery through the U.S.P.S. These competitors often accept packages that the U.S.P.S. will not accept, such as packages exceeding weight and size limitations imposed by the U.S.P.S.

Changes in Industry. — The last couple of decades have seen unprecedented change in the way people communicate with each other. In the 1990s most written communication was by letter, with specially urgent messages sent by telegram. Telephone conversations were conducted over landlines with each household typically having a single line all members had to share. Long distance conversations were limited in many households because of the high expense.

But with the rise of email, first-class mail, which peaked in 2001, has been steadily decreasing. Telegraphy is virtually non-existent. Western Union sent its last telegram on January 27, 2006.

What would Samuel Morse, inventor of the Morse Code, who sent the first telegram from Washington to Baltimore on May 26, 1844, think of the overwhelming number of choices we have today of how to communicate?

With just a cell phone, we can communicate with one another using words, images, voice, and video. We can type in text and send that by email or text. After taking a picture with the camera on our phone, we can send that in the same way. Or we can send a song that we have recorded or a video that we have shot.

We can receive communications containing text, images, voice, and video sent directly to us, or we can receive them as a follower of someone on social media, such as Twitter or Instagram.

We can establish two-way voice communications via phone and two-way video sessions using Skype.

Groups of people scattered around the globe can meet together using video conferencing software.

In two short decades we have gone from a household having a single landline shared by all members of the family, to a household where every member old enough to leave the house without supervision has his or her own cell phone, and the capabilities that go with it.

In the words of Samuel Morse's first telegram, "What hath God wrought?"

Broadcasting. — Broadcasting is the distribution of audio or video content from a single source to multiple listeners or viewers, typically using radio waves in the electromagnetic spectrum. Radio and television are the primary forms of this over the air transmission. Broadcasting services may be managed by the government, as in the case of public radio, community radio, and public television, or by private enterprise, as in the case of commercial radio and commercial television. In order to transmit their programs to their audiences, every radio and television station must have a broadcast license.

Federal Communications Commission. — In the United States it is the Federal Communications Commission that has the power to decide who can use which frequencies of the radio spectrum for which purposes, and issues licenses as necessary. Some obvious uses are AM radio, FM radio, and television stations, but there also many other uses, including short wave radio, citizens band radio, air traffic control, GPS, cell phones, cordless phones, garage door openers, baby monitors, and wildlife tracking collars. Each of these uses, and dozens of others, are assigned to their own band of the electromagnetic spectrum. When new parts of the spectrum become available for commercial use, the FCC holds auctions and awards different frequencies to the highest bidder. The FCC also regulates transmissions by wire and cable, so it exercises oversight over the wired telephone system and cable television.

QUESTIONS

1. Find out how much it would cost to mail a 10 pound box of books from your house to a distant city using media mail and USPS Retail Ground.

2. How much does it cost to mail a First-Class letter?

3. How many phones does your family have? What type are they?

4. How many devices do you have in your house that operate using radio waves in the electromagnetic spectrum?

5. What is meant by a money order? A passport? Certified mail?

6. What are the proper ways to send money by mail? Why?

CHAPTER XVII

FOREIGN AFFAIRS

Our Relations with Other Nations. — Our nation is so great, rich, and powerful that it might seem in no way dependent on any one else, that it could do what it pleased and get what it wished by its own strength. Yet this is not the case. Every nation, no matter how strong, is in some way dependent upon other countries and other parts of the world. It is a member of the family of nations, and it must exert itself to be in good relations with its neighbors. As we are polite and considerate to persons with whom we come in contact in our daily life, so nations should be considerate of one another. They should respect one another's rights and not do anything from a feeling of hostility or malice.

The Promotion of Commerce. — If we consider a little, we shall see how dependent we are upon other parts of the world in certain matters. In our daily life we need very many things which are not produced in our country. The products of the tropics like coconuts, rubber, precious woods like mahogany and ebony, articles of food like coffee and tea, are not produced in our country. Many other things which we need are not raised in sufficiently large quantities to satisfy our needs. For all these things we have to depend on others. We have to purchase them from the producers in other countries. There are also many manufactured articles which the people in foreign countries can make better or more cheaply than they can be produced here, so that we buy them from abroad. On the other hand, we desire to sell to the people of other countries the products of our factories and of our farms. In many lines we produce and manufacture more than we can use for ourselves. By selling the things we do not need to other nations, we secure money with which to buy foreign products which are necessary for our convenience or welfare. So we have many business relations with other countries. We also want some of our engineers to go to other parts of the world to build railways or bridges, or to set up great electrical plants for providing cities with light and power. If we all had to stay at home and confine our work and trade to our own country, we should lose many advantages.

Passports. — In order that all these activities may go on, our government makes agreements or treaties with other countries by which our commerce is protected and by which our citizens are permitted to travel freely and safely in foreign lands. Before leaving this country for foreign parts, an American citizen must obtain from the government a passport. This passport book is a document issued by the State Department, in which the name and a description of the bearer are given, and which calls upon a foreign government to afford him protection and other privileges. In other countries, should one desire the government to interfere in his behalf, he will show his passport and thus prove his right to protection. As we expect these favors from foreign governments, we should be hospitable to their citizens who come to our shores. Since 2008, passport cards the size of a credit card have been issued that allow cardholders to cross the United States border into and out of Bermuda, Canada, Mexico and some Caribbean countries by land or sea.

Diplomats. — In order that our interests and our citizens may be protected in foreign countries, our government has representatives stationed in all parts of the world. These are either diplomats or consuls. The diplomats — ambassadors, envoys, and ministers — represent the political interests of the nation. They report to our State Department about conditions in foreign countries, and when treaties are to be made, they represent our government. Great honor is accorded to diplomats because they are held to represent the majesty of their country. Their persons are sacred, and they cannot be arrested or interfered with in any manner by the foreign government.

Consuls. — The consuls are officials who look after the well-being of our citizens in other lands, as well as the commercial interests of our country. Activities of a consulate include protecting the interests of our citizens who are temporarily or permanently residing in the host country and issuing passports. Consulates also issue visas to foreigners and engage in public diplomacy. However, the principal role of a consulate lies traditionally in promoting trade—assisting companies to invest and to import and export goods and services between their home country and their host country. In every way the consuls will also protect and care for the interests of citizens traveling abroad. When one finds oneself in a foreign city, it is very pleasant to see the United States coat of arms above a doorway or to see the United States flag waving there. This indicates the home or office of a consul or diplomat. Americans are always welcome in such places, but they should be careful not to trouble the consuls, who are very busy persons, with private affairs, unless a real need exists.

The State Department. — All these officials are under the control of the Department of State, at the head of which is the highest official in the cabinet, the Secretary of State. This department watches over our interests in foreign countries. If the goods of American merchants are boycotted in China, the State Department will try to induce the Chinese government to protect our commerce. When a European country threatens to exclude our goods, the State Department will attempt to make a treaty by which their continued admission will be secured. These are examples of the many ways in which the State Department protects the interests of our commerce. But it is not only commerce, but every interest and pursuit of the American people, that the State Department makes its own and looks after in foreign lands.

Treaties. — When a treaty has been worked out by the Department of State and agreed to by the foreign government with which it is made, the President will submit it to the Senate. Under the Constitution, the

Senate must be consulted concerning every treaty, and no treaty will go into force without its approval. This gives the Senate great power over our foreign affairs. It is to be desired that while we stand up for our own interests and rights, we also respect those of other countries and be willing to work with them for the benefit of mankind.

QUESTIONS

1. Find out the procedure for applying for a U.S. passport.

2. What is the advantage of having a photograph attached to a passport?

3. What is the difference between an ambassador and a consul?

4. What is a "boycott"? Is it just?

5. How are treaties arranged? How ratified?

6. Define commerce; imports; exports; passport; diplomat; consul.

CHAPTER XVIII

THE MILITARY

Peace Assured. —The ordinary relations between the countries of the world are as peaceful as those between adjoining villages in our own country. It is desirable that nations should live in peace, should respect one another's rights, and should not give offense to one another. Peace brings happiness and prosperity. War means suffering, destruction, death. Our country is especially fortunate. We have no hostile neighbors who are seeking to attack us or who are jealous of our prosperity. The broad waters of the oceans, the Atlantic and the Pacific, protect our fair land from invasion.

Strength a Defense. — Every great nation in the world, however, must maintain its power, just as persons who may be perfectly peaceful and without desire to injure their neighbors in any way will still keep their bodies in good condition, strong and well. If the nation desires to be safe at all times, it must keep strong, so that no one will be tempted to take advantage of it. The army of the United States need not be large, for should a war arise it could be rapidly increased. If our nation should be attacked, the entire people would arise as one to defend their homes and their country. In peaceful times, therefore, a large army is unnecessary.

The Army. — The army of the United States at the present time numbers over one million soldiers, including those in the Reserve and the National Guard. The President is the commander-in-chief, but the Army is headed by a civilian who is appointed Secretary of the Army, and by a chief military officer, the Chief of Staff of the Army, who is a member of the Joint Chiefs of Staff. The Joint Chiefs of Staff are an important advisory body on military matters for the President, the Secretaries of Defense and Homeland Security, and the National Security Council.

In order that an army may be efficient, its officers must receive complete and thorough military education and training. For this purpose the government maintains a military academy at West Point on the Hudson. The ground is historic, dating from the Revolutionary War, the location is delightful, and the buildings and equipment provide for every need. Here young officer candidates selected for especial fitness, from all parts of the Union, are trained for four years in the art of war. The process of admission is so rigorous that an individual must meet the admissions requirements of the Academy as well as receive a nomination from a member of Congress in order to be offered an appointment. After a course of training extending over four years, the graduates of West Point are given a command in the army as lieutenants. The Army itself is recruited from volunteers; that is, no one is forced at the current time to serve in the Army, but those who like the life of the soldier may enlist. They are then paid for their service.

Militia.—In addition to the regular army of the United States there exists in each state bodies of troops called militias. Each state has two mandatory forces, the Army National Guard and the Air National Guard, which are reserve troops that may be called up for active duty by an individual state to help respond to emergencies or natural disasters and to civil disorder. Many states also have State Defense Forces and a naval militia, both of which aid and support the National Guard forces, but are separate from them. These are citizen soldiers that do not make a career of military service. They are people from all walks of life who frequently come together for the purpose of practicing military movements. In summer the militia assemble at a state camp, where they have special drills and maneuvers. The militia is the best kind of a military force for a republic. It keeps alive the training of the soldier, and at the same time it does not constitute a force which can be used against the liberties of the people. The regular army should never be made so large that the entire people could be oppressed by it.

The Navy. — The United States Navy is the largest navy in the world, with the largest aircraft carrier fleet and nearly five hundred thousand sailors, including the Navy Reserve. It was established during the Revolutionary War, played a major role in the Civil War, and was crucial in the defeat of Imperial Japan in World War II. Today The U.S. Navy has a significant global presence, in the Western Pacific, the Mediterranean, and the Indian Ocean, as well as in other locations. Being thus deployed it is able to respond quickly and with force to regional crises or threats throughout the world. A civilian Secretary of the Navy heads the Department of the Navy, along with a Chief of Naval Operations, who is the senior naval official of the Navy. The Department of the Navy, like the Army and the Air Force, is a division of the Department of Defense, answerable to the Secretary of Defense.

The Naval Academy. — It requires great skill and experience to command and control a modern battle ship. Those who manage its intricate machinery must be carefully trained. The government has therefore established a Naval Academy at Annapolis, Maryland, where sailors are thoroughly educated and trained in everything pertaining to naval warfare. Like the Army office candidates, candidates for the U.S. Naval Academy must be nominated by a member of Congress, though even that does not guarantee an appointment to Annapolis. Students are officers-in-training and called "midshipmen." Graduates of the Naval Academy are usually commissioned as ensigns in the Navy or second lieutenants in the United States Marine Corps to fulfill their active-duty service obligation.

The Marine Corps. — Another branch of the U.S. Armed Forces, which is closely allied with the Navy, is the United States Marine Corps. Despite being a smaller division than the other U.S. Armed Forces, with around two hundred thousand personnel, nevertheless it has become a major force in the execution of U.S. foreign policy. The Marine Corps is dominant in conducting amphibious warfare, and is versatile enough to deploy with short notice in response to crises all over the world. Its well-trained troops are capable of operating on land, air, and sea, often providing support for the other Armed Forces. The Corps is a division of the Department of the Navy, and its most senior official is the Commandant, who is a member of the Joint Chiefs of Staff, and is answerable to the Secretary of the Navy.

The Air Force. — The United States Air Force is the last branch of the Armed Forces which reports to the Department of Defense. Initially part of the U.S. Army, it is also the most recently-formed of the Armed Forces. As the largest and one of the most technologically advanced Air Forces in the world, it provides air support for ground and naval forces and helps recover troops in the field. While its service academy, the U.S. Air Force Academy in Colorado Springs, Colorado, is the youngest academy of the Armed Forces, its admissions standards are just as rigorous as those of the older academies. Graduates of the Air Force Academy are commissioned as second lieutenants in the U.S. Air Force.

The Coast Guard. — The fifth and final branch of the U.S. Armed Forces is the United States Coast Guard, the only military force under the command of the Department of Homeland Security. The smallest of the Armed Forces, the Coast Guard has around 23,000 active members. The Coast Guard has a variety of missions, with its Search and Rescue operations at sea the one for which it is best known. Coast Guardsmen also patrol the coast, keep aids to navigation in good working order, enforce fishing regulations, and monitor spills of oil, chemicals, and others substances on land as well as sea. With a decentralized organization and much responsibility placed on even junior Guardsmen, the Coast Guard is frequently praised for its ability to respond quickly to a broad range of emergencies.

QUESTIONS

1. What are the five branches of the Armed Forces and how do their responsibilities differ?

2. What qualifications for admission are demanded of those applying to the different service academies?

3. Under what conditions is war justifiable?

4. Tell something of your state militia.

CHAPTER XIX

TAXATION

The Expenses of Government. — In the preceding chapters we have seen the various ways in which the government acts on behalf of the people. We have seen how it defends and protects them against foreign attack and internal disorder. We have seen how it carries and distributes the mail, how it provides for education, how it develops the natural wealth of the country in forests and agricultural lands. For most of these advantages the people benefited do not pay directly. The government practically provides them freely in order to advance the general interest. All these things, however, cost a great deal of money, and hence the expenses of government are very great. This money is raised by taxation of one kind or another, and comes indirectly from all the people.

Oppressive Taxation. — In early times taxation could hardly be distinguished from robbery. We have already seen how dependent the peasant of the valley was upon the lord of the castle. This lord took not only what the peasants could produce, but he would also prey upon the merchants who traveled through his territory.

On the river Rhine, for instance, the lords of the castles would often stretch chains across the river and detain merchant vessels until they had paid an exaction or tax to the lord, who had really done nothing whatever for them. It is different in a modern civilized community. There the tax is a payment for service rendered by the government in protection, education, the development of resources, and the administration of law.

Forms of Taxation at the Federal Level. — The money needed by the federal government for rendering service to the public is collected through fees and various forms of taxation, including income tax, payroll tax, excise tax, and estate tax.

Fees. — We must distinguish between a fee and a tax. When a specific payment is made for a service by the government, it is called a fee. For a passport book or card one pays a certain fee. For having a letter registered or certified, the writer pays a different fee. But most of the services performed by the federal government are not paid for directly in this manner but by taxation.

Income Tax. — An income tax is a tax on one's taxable income. Taxable income is gross income less deductions. Gross income includes all income earned or received from any source. This includes salaries and wages, tips, pensions, rents and interest received, as well as many other types of income. The amount of tax paid is a percentage of the taxable income, with the rate determined by the income level. The rate of tax at the federal level is graduated, that is, the rate on higher amounts of income is higher than the rate on lower amount of income. Federal tax rates in a recent year ranged from 10% for the lowest level of income to 39.6% for the highest level of income.

Payroll Tax. — The FICA tax is a federal payroll tax imposed on both employers and employees to fund Social Security and Medicare, which are federal programs that provide benefits to retired persons, persons with disabilities, and children of workers who have died. The employer pays one half of these taxes and the employee the other half. Currently employees pay a tax of 6.2% for Social Security and a tax of 1.45% for Medicare.

Excise Tax. — Another source of federal revenue is found in the excise duties on items like gasoline, diesel fuel, tires, airline tickets, tobacco, and alcohol. This tax is paid by the manufacturer of the article, who typically adds it to the price, so that the consumer pays for it indirectly.

Estate Tax. — The estate tax is a tax on the transfer of the estate of a person who has died. At the federal level, only estates valued at greater than $5.45 million pay any estate tax.

Sources of Income to the Federal Government. —

Individual income taxes contribute 50% of total revenue to the federal budget, payroll taxes 33%, corporate income taxes 10%, and excise, estate, and other taxes contributing the remaining 7%.

Expenditures at the Local Level. People living in cities and towns must pay for the services their local governments provide. For example, residents pay for the maintenance of streets and public transportation in order that they may drive or ride in comfort. They pay for the service of police officers to watch over their safety day and night, and Emergency Medical Technicians (EMTs) to provide aid in a health emergency. They pay for the care of the parks where the children may play, and for the schools where children get their education. They pay for the service of firefighters to protect property, and sanitation engineers to handle their waste and collect their recycling. All of these services, and many others besides, add to the expenses of local government.

Forms of Taxation at the State and Local Level. — The money needed by state and local governments for rendering service to the public is collected through fees and various forms of taxation, including sales tax, property tax, income tax, and estate tax. Types of taxes and tax rates vary from one state to another, and from one locality to another.

Fees. — States and local governments derive revenue from license fees collected from business-owners, automobile drivers and others.

Sales Tax. — A sales tax is a tax paid to a governing body for sales of certain goods and services. It is typically collected at the time the items are sold at retail. Forty-five states have a sales tax that applies to most goods. Many states also grant authority to local governments to impose additional sales taxes. The sales tax is calculated by multiplying the purchase price by the applicable tax rate. Tax rates vary by locality and range from less than

1% to over 10%. Some states exempt food, clothing, and prescriptions from sales tax to lessen the burden on residents buying essential goods.

Property Tax. — Most local governments in the United States have property taxes on real estate as a principal source of revenue. This tax on land and buildings is nearly always computed as the fair market value of the property times an assessment ratio times a tax rate. Property values are determined by local officials and may be disputed by property owners. Periodically an officer known as the assessor looks over all the property in the town or city. The assessor determines the value of all real estate. When the assessment roll has been made up, the taxes which the people in a given locality have to pay are apportioned among the residents according to their property values. If property owners are not satisfied, and think the assessor has put too high a valuation on their property, they can ask to have their assessment reviewed. When the day of payment comes, the assessed tax must be paid. The state is not a creditor that can be put off. If one should fail to pay the tax assessed upon one's property, it would be sold at public auction by the sheriff, in order that the state might receive its tax. For this reason, people are more anxious to pay their property taxes promptly than to meet any other obligation.

Personal Property Tax. — Some state and local governments also tax tangible personal property, namely property that can be transported. This tax, though, constitutes a relatively small source of income for state and local government.

Income Tax. — Forty-three states impose an income tax on their residents. Local governments can also impose an income tax on residents who live or work with their borders.

Estate Tax and Inheritance Tax. — Estate taxes and inheritance taxes vary from one state to another. Fourteen states have estate taxes that are paid from the estate of the deceased. Like the federal estate tax, only estates valued at greater than a certain amount (ranging from $1 million to $5.49 million at the state level) pay any estate tax. Six states have an inheritance tax which is paid by the heirs of the deceased. A surviving spouse is exempt from inheritance tax in all states. A deceased person's children may be taxed at a lower rate. Of course, when there are no relatives at all to inherit the property, it will fall to the state.

Sources of Income to State and Local Governments. — On average, property taxes contribute 35% of total revenue to state and local budgets, sales taxes 34%, individual income taxes 20%, corporate income taxes 3%, motor vehicle license fees 2%, with other taxes contributing the remaining 6%.

Cost of State and Local Governments. — The expenses of the state and local governments are, of course, somewhat smaller than the cost of the federal government. At the present time they amount to about $2.7 trillion per year.

QUESTIONS

1. What is the rate of taxation on real estate where you live?

2. What are the largest items of expenditure in your local budget?

3. Is there an inheritance tax in your state? Is there an estate tax? If so, what are their terms?

4. How is the tax on tobacco paid?

5. What does your schooling cost the city or town each year?

6. Is church and college property taxed in your state? Is this just?

7. Is there a sales tax where you live? If so, what is the rate and what products are exempted, if any?

8. Should a wealthy person who has no children be obliged to pay towards the support of schools? Why?

CHAPTER XX

LEGISLATION

The Making of Laws. — We have considered the many activities of the state, the manner in which it acts on behalf of the people, and in which it provides itself with funds for its expenses. We have seen hundreds of thousands of officials at work in their various departments looking after the interests of the people and advancing the welfare of the country. There must be somewhere a body of persons who will make rules according to which all these officials act and according to which the citizens are protected and have their interests guarded by the government. In the state the body which makes these rules is the legislature, and in the nation it is Congress. In smaller divisions rules are made by the county boards, city councils, village boards, and town meetings. But in the state all such councils and boards are subordinate to the state legislature, which can prescribe rules of action even to these bodies.

Civil and Criminal Laws. — The legislature of the state frames the general rules by which the citizens must regulate their conduct. This is called the civil and criminal law of the state. Our moral sense tells us that we must not do bodily injury to another person nor take from him what rightfully is his or her own. Upon this moral sense the legislature bases the law which protects life and property and punishes crimes committed against citizens. These laws also lay down general rules for business transactions and the holding and transfer of property. It is a law that when I agree in writing to purchase $10,000 worth of lumber, I must carry out my promise. All these and many similar rules deal with the conduct of private citizens in respect to their general affairs.

Rules for Officials. — The second kind of rules made by the legislature deals with the action of government officials, prescribing regulations according to which they must do their work. Thus, the laws will instruct the Secretary of State how certificates of incorporation are to be issued. They will provide on what conditions insurance companies will be permitted to do business in a state. They will instruct the game wardens and the foresters as to their duties. The legislature also has control over all the expenditures of the state. No official is permitted to pay out any state money if the legislature has not previously given its consent to such expenditure. As the legislature is elected directly by the people, we see how all officials are under the control of the electors. If the citizens will only interest themselves in political matters and have a definite purpose, they will be able to impress their desires upon the government of the country.

Power of Congress. — The Congress of the United States has no control over the ordinary rules determining the conduct of citizens. The laws of contract, of property, of crime, are made by the state legislatures and not by Congress. The national body deals with the work of federal government and with such matters as are provided for in the Constitution of the United States.

Congress has power over the financial and budgetary concerns of the government. Most of the acts of Congress deal with the established services of the departments of the government, and all of its expenditures.

How a Law is Made. — It is very interesting to observe the work of a legislative body. The legislature represents the different parties existing among the people of the state or nation. These parties discuss questions of public interest, and their members struggle to secure influence and power. When a member of the legislature desires to have a new law passed, he or she frames a bill; that is, the legislator writes out what the proposal is in the form of a law. This bill the legislator introduces on the floor of the House. The Speaker of the House will then send it to a committee. It is impossible for the House itself to go over all the bills which are proposed by members. They must first be examined and sifted by one of the many committees into which the House is divided. Thus, if the bill calls for an appropriation of money, it will be referred to the Appropriations Committee. If it provides for the repair and reconstruction of bridges, it will go to the Committee that handles Transportation and Infrastructure issues. These are a couple of examples. There are dozens of committees in the houses of the legislatures of the various states.

A citizen who has an interest in any matter of legislation may contact his or her legislator in a number of ways:

1. Call the legislator's office and make an appointment to discuss a particular issue.

2. Attend a Town Hall meeting.

3. Write a letter to the legislator to express one's views.

4. Send an e-mail message expressing one's views.

5. Call the legislative hotline to leave a message on any issue.

6. Testify before a committee that is holding public hearings on an issue or bill. Hearings are announced ahead of time so that citizens who are interested can be present.

Persons who make it a business to secure legislation for others, who pay them for their efforts, are called lobbyists. If they simply argue openly before committees, there is nothing wrong about their work, but if they try secretly to influence legislators, their action is illegal. In most states lobbyists are obliged by law to register their name and that of their employer.

If the committee finds that it would be desirable to pass a certain bill, it will report this bill to the House with its recommendation. The bill is then put to a vote; those favoring it will say "Aye," those against it, "No." If a majority of the members present vote for the bill, it is passed. In some states a majority of all the members belonging to the House must vote favorably in order to pass a measure. When the bill is thus passed in one branch, it will be sent to the other — each legislature having two branches. There it goes through the same process. If it is passed by the second branch, it will be sent to the governor for his approval, and thus becomes a law.

Veto Power. — The governor has the right to veto a bill if he considers it undesirable. Veto is a Latin word meaning "I forbid." Sometimes the legislature may have overlooked some defect in the law, or the members may have become excited and passed a measure that in the light of reason seems dangerous to the state, or the legislature may have gone beyond the powers given to it by the constitution. In these cases the governor will usually exercise the power of veto. This veto does not necessarily defeat the bill. It goes back to the legislature. If this body passes it again, with an enlarged majority, — two thirds in most states, — the bill becomes a law notwithstanding the governor's veto. The legislature need not accept the opinion of the governor on the character of the law. In such a case the people will judge between the legislature and the governor, and uphold whichever in their opinion takes the right view of the case.

The Initiative and Referendum. — The constitutions of many states at the present time provide that, when a large number of voters desire to have a certain law enacted, they may bring it before the people of the state by an initiative petition. When this has been done, a vote will be had on the proposed law at the next regular election. Should a law passed by the legislature appear to a large number of voters unwise and undesirable, they may petition for its reference to the electorate (referendum). When such a petition has been signed by the required number of voters, the law to which it refers will not go into operation before it has been voted on by the general electorate. This method makes it possible for the people of a state to keep very direct control over legislation, and themselves to make the laws which they desire to have enacted, when the legislature does not readily respond to the determined will of the people.

QUESTIONS

1. Have you ever seen a legislative body in session? Describe its appearance.

2. Who currently represents your district in your state's House and Senate? In Congress?

3. What is a veto? A civil law? A lobby? A lobbyist?

4. Define legislature; criminal laws; Congress; Constitution.

5. What powers has Congress? The state legislature?

8. Who presides over the Senate? The House of Representatives? Name these officers during the current session of Congress.

PART III

The Organization of the Government

CHAPTER XXI

THE TOWN AND VILLAGE

Local Government. — As we know most about the needs of our own neighborhood, it is natural that we should pay most attention to these and manage them ourselves as much as possible. We should know about the affairs of the state and nation, but management of them we must entrust to representatives and officials. The affairs of our town, village, or city, however, are so close to us, and we are so directly responsible for them, that it is our special duty and privilege to see that they are well administered.

The Town-meeting. — In some of our states, notably in New England and the midwest, — the people living in country districts are governed by the town-meeting. In New England the town is a small settlement, often dating back to the very beginning of our history. To the town belong the adjoining lands, and its boundaries are the irregular lines inclosing them, the whole territory forming a township. In other states the townships are more artificial. They are often square areas determined by the calculations of surveyors, who went through our newer states and laid them out into counties and towns.

In some of these newer states also the towns have their town-meetings. At least one town-meeting is held each year, in addition to which extra meetings may be held. At these meetings each citizen of the town has a right to be present, speak, and vote. A citizen with a proper sense of his or her own interests and duties, will not fail to be present on these occasions. The town-meeting elects the town officers, and passes regulations called by-laws.[1]

Township Government. — In the townships of the states in which no town-meetings are held, the work of the town is conducted entirely by officials elected by citizens of the town. The general business of the town may be managed by selectmen, trustees, or supervisors. Of the latter there is usually only one to each town, but in New England towns there may be from three to nine selectmen. These officials control and carry out the general administration of public affairs in the town, though where a town-meeting exists, they are subject to its orders. They fix the rate of taxation, vote money for expenses, and control the other officials, such as the clerk, the treasurer, the assessor, the tax collector, the constable or sheriff, the justice of the peace, and the superintendents of highways. The duties of these various officials are indicated by their title. The clerk keeps the books of the town, the records of town-meeting; he or she issues notices and frames the various

[1]"Town" comes from the Anglo-Saxon *"tun,"* referring to the fence or palisade built about towns in ancient times for protection. *By* is the Norse word for town. A by-law, therefore, means a town law. England, as you remember, was settled both by Anglo-Saxons and by Norsemen.

written instruments necessary in town government. The treasurer has charge of the town funds. The assessor determines the value of property in the town for the purposes of taxation. The constable or sheriff is the peace officer who has the power of making arrests and serving warrants. By holding offices of this kind, the citizens learn the public business of the town, so that it is an advantage both to themselves and to the state that they should render this service. In doing so they are fulfilling a public duty.

Village Government. — As the town settlement increases in population, the village comes into being. Farmers of the neighborhood who have been successful retire and build themselves houses in the village. New stores are opened, warehouses and lumber yards and even factories may be added, so that the village presents an aspect of far greater business activity than does a country settlement. The people living in a village, therefore, find it necessary to exercise powers which are not required in the case of a town. They need special regulations concerning streets, sidewalks, fire, water supply, sewerage, and other matters. The state will, therefore, grant to villages a charter under which these extended powers may be exercised by the citizens of the village. In general, the government is similar to that of a town, but the powers are greater, and the designation of the officials is different. At the head of the village is the president. The by-laws of the village are made by the board of trustees, which also supervises the public business, levies taxes, and appropriates money for public expenses. Generally a village is a part of a town, so that the citizens of the village also have the right to vote for town officers.

QUESTIONS

1. Do you live in a town where there are town meetings? What are the powers of the town meeting?

2. What are the officials of your town or village?

3. What are the duties of a supervisor or trustee?

4. What is the duty of the town clerk? Who has charge of the highways?

5. What advantages has a town over a city?

6. Define town; village; charter; assessor; justice of the peace.

CHAPTER XXII

THE CITY

What is a City? — As more and more people settle in a village, it gradually grows into a city. It is important that we should understand all that is meant by the word "city." It is not merely a large number of houses located near each other, an area covered with streets and buildings, or a mass of people. It means more than all this. A city has a life of its own, a character which is developed by the experience of time like the character of an individual person.

In the ancient world, when Greece and Rome were powerful, the city was even more important than it is today. At that time there was nothing above the city. It was the highest political unit. Consider for a moment the appearance of an ancient city. On a high hill were seen the shining walls and the gleaming roofs of temples and public halls. Standing among them were giant statues of marble, ivory, or gold representing the gods to whom the city was faithful. Upon the top of the cliffs that formed the sides of the citadel ran massive walls of masonry protecting the temples. On the lower slopes of the hill there were amphitheaters, more temples, public markets, and the dwellings of the citizens. All about the city was constructed another strong wall for the purpose of defense. Beyond this there lay the fields tilled by the citizens and their dependents. This city was to the people of the age their home, church, country, their everything. If they had to leave it, they were strangers, without peace or rest. Only in their own city were they free persons. They loved their city with a personal love. The picture of its walls and temples impressed itself so clearly upon the mind that all its outlines could be recalled at any time. As you know the appearance of your home, so the ancient citizen carried with him the picture of his city wherever he went. These cities were governed by the citizens in public meetings. They would not acknowledge any political superior.

Italian Cities. — Should we travel in Italy today, we should see many cities which remind us of these ancient cities, and which, in fact, are in many respects like them. Each Italian city — Florence, Venice, Milan, Rome, Naples — has its own character, different from that of any other. The style of its buildings, the appearance of its inhabitants, show these differences. These cities are proud of the fine and dignified appearance of their public buildings, their squares and streets. We shall see, by thinking of these matters, that the cities have been the places where in the past our civilization has developed and has had its centers. It is there that freedom was born because, under the protection of the city walls, the citizens felt a sense of freedom and equality which the unprotected person in the country could not feel.

American Cities. — Our American cities are not so picturesque nor do they have as much individual character as have these older cities of which we have spoken, but they, too, are more than mere crowds of people. It is remarkable how fast our cities have grown. In the year 1800 there was not one city in America which had one hundred thousand inhabitants. At that time our population lived in country districts, and was occupied largely in farming, but during the last two centuries great manufacturing enterprises, retail establishments, and office complexes were built up and the business of the country was centered in a number of large cities. People of all sorts came to live in larger and larger numbers in the cities, so that today 70% of our population is found in cities of over 50,000 inhabitants.

Cosmopolitan Cities. — Our American cities are also notable because of the many people of foreign descent who live in them and make their population greatly diverse. In the early years of our history, country districts were usually settled by people of some one nationality, — English, German, Scandinavian, Polish, or some other nationality. But in the cities peoples of various nationalities live side by side. In the public schools of New York City today, over 170 languages are spoken. Our country has been hospitable in welcoming a variety of peoples to our shores. For this reason our population has grown very fast. It is not surprising that many of these immigrants stay in the large cities, where work may easily be secured and land is hard to obtain. This fact makes the government of our large cities more challenging than that of foreign cities in an earlier era where the people all spoke the same language and shared many of the same customs.

Cities Beautified. — The city ought to be made a dignified and beautiful home for its inhabitants. By the cities our civilization will be judged. If they are corrupt, if their streets and buildings are unattractive, we have much still to do. But they need not be other than beautiful and well governed if the people will only discharge their duties as citizens. Many of our American cities, indeed, may be looked upon already as models of what a city should be. They have clean, well-paved streets lined with welcome shade trees; public squares, flanked with impressive buildings; libraries, museums, city halls, and schools of ample size and artistic design. They honor their distinguished citizens by monuments erected to them in appropriate places. While all such improvements as these are expensive, they are an excellent investment, because they make the city a pleasanter place for all its residents.

City Charter. — The government of the city is carried on under a charter, a grant of powers made by the legislature. The city is a larger town or village, with a greater population and a greater variety of activities. It needs greater powers of government and a more complicated organization than a village.

The Mayor of the City. — At the head of the city government stands the mayor. He or she has the power of appointing certain officials, of watching over the execution of laws, of suggesting new ordinances to the city council. A city's mayor generally has the right to veto ordinances passed by that body. The executive work of the city is carried out by numerous officials and boards which are grouped in various city departments. The arrangement and designation of these vary in different parts of the country. There will be city treasurers, auditors, boards for the management of streets, parks, the police, the water supply, and the school system. If we live in a city, we ought to know the various departments of the city government and their business. We could then see how each one successfully carries on its work.

The City Council. — The ordinances or laws of the city are made by the council. This city legislature may be composed of one or two bodies. Most commonly it has only one body. The city legislators are usually called aldermen or alderwomen. Their powers of legislation are granted in the charter. The council may make certain rules with respect to the use of the streets and of the parks, as well as regulations controlling the work of the city officials. It also deals with the income and expenses of the city. The income is derived from taxes on property, from rentals and fees for public services such as the water supply, and from the return from franchises granted to public service corporations. The city may borrow money for the purpose of constructing public buildings and works of various kinds, but the amount of indebtedness which a city can incur is limited by law. This precaution is taken in order that the council may not run into debt recklessly. Generally the debt of a city is fixed at a percentage of the assessed valuation of all the property in the city.

QUESTIONS

1. Give the names of the departments of your city government, and describe their work.

2. What important officials are appointed by the mayor of your city?

3. How is the work of street maintenance organized?

4. How large a debt does your city have?

5. What has been done towards beautifying your city or town?

6. Attend a meeting of the council and report its proceedings to your classmates.

7. Give some suggestions for improving the appearance of your city or town.

8. Why do so many foreign immigrants settle in our cities?

9. How does an immigrant become a voting citizen?

10. Name five of the largest cities in your state and give their population.

11. Who is the mayor of your city? What powers has the mayor?

12. What are the powers and duties of the city council?

CHAPTER XXIII

THE COUNTY

What is a County? — The county is a district or division of government which exists in all states of the Union, with the exception of Louisiana, where the district or local government is called a parish, and in Alaska where it is called a borough. Where the town meeting is very active, as in New England, the county is far less important. In the Southern states and in the Far West, however, where town government does not exist, the county performs all the work of local administration. The county is a division of the state created for the purpose of carrying on certain public business.

County Government. — The county is governed by a board of county commissioners or supervisors. The county commissioners are usually chosen for the entire county, while the board of supervisors is made up of representatives from each town and each ward in a city or village. Consequently, a board of supervisors is much larger than a board of county commissioners. Whatever the system may be in a given county, the powers of the board are similar. It apportions the state tax among the various towns, villages, and cities in the county, equalizing the tax assessments when any inequalities exist. The construction and care of courthouses, jails, and other public buildings also devolve upon this body. It may also exercise supervision over the system of roads and over public education in the county.

County Officers. — The usual county officers are the clerk, the treasurer, the register of deeds, the county school superintendent, the sheriff, and the district attorney or state's attorney. All these officials are elected by the voters of the county. The register of deeds keeps a record of all landed property in the county. Whenever a piece of land is sold or mortgaged, the deed or mortgage is recorded by the register. In this way the transfer of the property is made public, and the purchaser is assured of getting a good title to the land bought. Should there be any mortgage on the land, or should any sale have been previously made, the record at the courthouse plainly shows the fact. The sheriff is an important official whose duty it is to secure the enforcement of law and the maintenance of order throughout the county. A county's sheriff has the power of making arrests, and also serves as the custodian of the persons who are confined in the county jail.

QUESTIONS

1. How large is the county board in your county?

2. How large is the governing body of your county, and how is it designated?

3. Name the officers of your county.

4. What buildings belong to it, and where are they located?

5. Is every state divided into counties? What is a parish? A borough?

6. What are the duties of the county commissioners or supervisors?

7. Name the county seat of your county. Why chosen and when?

8. How many counties are in your state? Name the largest county in your state and the smallest.

9. If you bought a farm in your county, where and to what county officer would you go to have your title recorded?

CHAPTER XXIV

THE STATE GOVERNMENT

Importance of State Government. — When the United States government was founded, there existed only thirteen states, but these states had in their possession a large tract of territory extending to the Mississippi River which had not yet been settled. As the settlement extended into these new lands and as the population there grew, new states were formed and admitted into the Union. It was not long before this original territory had thus been settled and formed into states. This same line of action continued when the federal government acquired the far western territory, and the territories of Alaska and Hawaii.

The government of the state is very important to our general welfare. President Garfield once described it in the following language: — "The state government touches the citizen and his interests twenty times where the national government touches him once. For the peace of our streets and the health of our cities; for the administration of justice in nearly all that relates to the security of person and property, and the punishment of crime; for the education of our children, and the care of unfortunate and dependent citizens; for the collection and assessment of much the larger portion of our direct taxes, and for the proper expenditure of the same, — for all this, and much more, we depend upon the honesty and wisdom of our General Assembly and not upon the Congress at Washington."

State Insignia. — Each state has an individuality of its own. It not only has its name, but also its seal and its coat of arms. A coat of arms originally was the covering which a knight wore over his armor and upon which was embroidered a shield. Upon this there were represented various objects supposed to be connected with the character and history of the family of the knight. This coat of arms was inherited by son from father. Though armed and plumed knights have long passed away, coats of arms are still used to indicate somewhat the character of a family or a state. In selecting the coats of arms of our states, our forefathers tried to express their hopes and aspirations. They placed upon them not the fierce lions and tigers which abounded on the coats of arms of the ancient warriors. Our designs are usually in every way peaceful. The plow, the anvil, the locomotive, the steamship, and other means of promoting the wellbeing of mankind have taken the place of swords and beasts of prey. These coats of arms are found in the center of the great seal of the state. Some of the states have a separate state flag or banner, or they may have selected certain flowers, trees, or birds to represent them. Nearly all the states have a motto. Among the people, humorous designations are often given to states and their inhabitants, such as buckeye

(Ohio), badger (Wisconsin), gopher (Minnesota), hoosier (Indiana), etc.

Equality of States. — In law all the states of the Union, large and small, are equal, and cannot be interfered with by another state or by the federal government, but in actual size they vary greatly. The largest state, Alaska, is over 10 times as large as Illinois, and Illinois again is forty times as large as Rhode Island, the smallest state.

The Constitution of the State. — In the United States, each state has its own constitution. Typically state constitutions address a wide array of issues deemed by the states to be of sufficient importance to be included in the constitution rather than in an ordinary statute. Often modeled after the federal Constitution, they outline the structure of the state government and typically establish a bill of rights (often called Declaration of Rights), an executive branch headed by a governor (and often one or more other officials, such as a lieutenant governor and state attorney general), a state legislature, and state courts, including a state supreme court (a few states have two high courts, one for civil cases, the other for criminal cases). They also provide a general governmental framework for what each branch is supposed to do and how it should go about doing it. The constitution may be changed in parts and in detail by amendments. These amendments are proposed by the state legislature, and are then submitted to the people to be voted upon at a regular election. The constitution contains the general framework of government. It enumerates the departments of government and distributes the powers among them. It also forbids the exercise of certain powers. It regulates the right of voting, and determines what shall be necessary in order that citizens may hold office.

The Governor. — The work of the state is carried on in the counties by the officials and boards which we have already considered. The central government of the state is composed of the governor, the executive officers, the legislature, and the state courts. The governor represents the unity of state government. He or she may appoint certain officials, usually with the consent of the Senate, in the case of important appointments. At present, in some states, appointments are made not as a matter of political favor, but on the basis of civil service examinations. All candidates for a certain office have the right to be examined, and appointment must be made from those who stand highest on the list and have passed the test with the greatest credit to themselves.

Over 20 states have volunteer state guard units. These units, formally known as state defense forces (SDFs), are today's state militias. In most states the governor is also the commander of the state defense forces. Should great disorders or rioting arise in any part of the state, the governor may call out the state defense forces to restore order.

The governor usually has the power to pardon persons who have been sentenced to prison or to other forms of punishment. When a sentence has once been passed by a court, it has no power to discharge the accused. It is sometimes discovered, however, after the trial, that a prisoner is really innocent of the crime of which he or she was convicted. If the prisoner's innocence is clearly established, the governor may issue a pardon. This great power should, however, not be used to allow prisoners to escape the just punishment for their crime.

Perhaps the most important function of the governor is the preparation of a message which he or she sends to the legislature or reads before it in person. In this message the governor recommends such changes in the law as seem necessary. As a person of power and wisdom, the governor will be able greatly to influence the action of the legislature. When an act has been passed by the legislature, it must be submitted to the governor, who has the right either to approve it or to veto it. In case it is vetoed, it may still become a law if the legislature passes it again. In most states, however, the act must be re-passed in such a case by a vote larger than a simple majority.

Executive Officers. — The executive work of the state is carried on by various officials. The most important of these are the secretary of state, the treasurer, the attorney-general, the superintendent of education, and the auditor. The secretary of state keeps the record of all the laws and important public acts of state government. The great seal of the state, which must be affixed to the original copy of every law, is in the custody of the secretary of state.

Boards and Commissions. — Boards and commissions are independent bodies consisting of private citizens appointed by public officials, usually the governor. Boards and commissions are designed to give individuals a voice in their government and provide a means of influencing decisions that shape the quality of life for the state's residents. Participation on a board or commission is one of the most effective steps citizens can take in becoming an active voice in their government. Many states have hundreds of boards and commissions dealing with virtually every state department and public policy area. So states welcome applications to serve on boards and commissions from persons with demonstrated interest and expertise in relevant areas. Boards and commissions are of two types: some are regulatory and others are advisory. Regulatory boards have the right to make rules and regulations which officials and residents must observe. They may oversee licensing, handle complaints, and enforce disciplinary actions with regard to issues under their authority. Advisory boards explore questions from all sides, then make recommendations to public officials, including the governor, legislature, and state agencies, on particular issues. Consider the public service commission as an example. It typically has the power to determine whether the rates proposed by utility companies for their services are just and reasonable.

State Legislatures. — The legislature of the state consists of two houses in every state but Nebraska. The smaller house is called the Senate, the larger, the House of Representatives. In some states the latter is called the House of Delegates or the Assembly. The senators are elected from districts which are larger, and their term of office is usually longer than that of the representatives. The House of Representatives is sometimes three times as large as the Senate. While the senators are ordinarily elected for four years, the representatives are elected for two years only. Of course, every state has its own system in these matters, so that we are here simply stating the arrangements which have been made in most of the states.

The presiding officer in the House of Representatives is called the speaker. The Senate is presided over either by the lieutenant governor or one of the senators who acts as president. In both houses the detailed work is carried on in committees. These are called standing committees when they are regularly appointed at each session, and select or special committees when they are appointed for a short time and for a special purpose. The most important standing committees are those dealing with revenue and expenditure, with education, with health, with transportation, with elections, with commerce, and with agriculture. Every bill which is introduced must be referred to a committee, and unless the committee makes a favorable report on it, it is not likely that the bill will become a law. The speaker has the power of appointing committees and of maintaining order in the House. Any member who desires to address the House must first catch the eye of the speaker and obtain recognition from him.

In 46 states the legislature meets annually, but there are four states in which the legislature meets every two years. The length of the session is limited by law in most states. It is believed to be wise for the legislature to work with a will and to finish up its business in as short a time as possible. Should any important matter come up after the legislature has adjourned, the governor may call an extra session.

State Courts. — The work of the state courts deals with the ordinary personal and property rights of citizens as well as with criminal acts committed against the state itself. Whenever only the rights of a private individual are dealt with, we speak of a "civil" action ; a "criminal" action takes place when an offense has been committed that is serious enough to affect public peace and security in general. In such cases we say that the act has been committed against the peace of the state or commonwealth. The manner of dealing with these various kinds of cases has already been described above. State courts are divided into the following classes: Justice courts for the trial of cases of small importance; probate courts for the proving of wills, the administration of estates, and the guardianship of minor children; courts of general civil and criminal jurisdiction; and courts of appeal, or supreme courts, to which cases are brought when the decision of a lower court is objected to. The judges of state courts are usually elected by popular vote, or appointed by the Governor; it is important that good and experienced judges should be kept in service as long as possible.

QUESTIONS

1. What is the design of the great seal of your state?

2. Does your state have a flag, a motto, a state flower, a state bird, a state tree?

3. Read the Declaration of Rights in your state constitution, and see how it protects personal rights against interference.

4. How often does the legislature meet in your state?

CHAPTER XXV

THE NATIONAL GOVERNMENT

The National Capital. — Our national capital is one of the most beautiful cities in the world. The site upon which it stands was selected by George Washington himself. He was fond of this region, because nearby is situated his own estate of Mount Vernon. Before a single building was constructed, a skilled engineer drew up a complete plan for the city, showing all the streets, avenues, and parks which were to be created.

The Capitol. — The city really has two centers, if such a thing is possible. On an eminence in the eastern part of the city stands the Capitol, surmounted by its majestic dome. You have so often seen a picture of this noble building that you have perhaps ceased to care for it. But look at it again and see how beautiful it is. Its vast size does not surprise you, but all its parts are so constructed that they are in perfect harmony with each other. It is not the size of a building which makes its beauty, but perfect proportions, — that is, the relation of its parts and its lines to one another, so that the effect will be entirely harmonious. But while its lines

135

make the building beautiful, its size makes it impressive. Where the two go together, a very powerful impression is produced. So with the vast stairway sweeping up towards the building, with its marble wings extended on either side, and the perfectly fashioned dome crowning the entire structure, it may be said there is no building in the world more fit to represent national strength and permanence than the Capitol in Washington. It is surrounded by other magnificent structures, the Library of Congress, the Supreme Court building, and the office buildings for Congress. In arranging such great structures it is always necessary to leave sufficient space around them in order that they may not be crowded and that they may not detract from one another.

The White House. — Pennsylvania Avenue leads westward from the Capitol. It is a broad street, the principal thoroughfare of Washington. It leads up to the White House, the official home of the President, a simple building surrounded by beautiful park-like gardens. In front of the White House is Lafayette Square, a place of great historical interest. In its center is a statue of Andrew Jackson, the soldier President. The square itself is surrounded by houses in which have lived such men as James Madison, Daniel Webster, Charles Sumner, John Hay, Admiral Decatur, and others famous in our history.

The National Mall. — Centrally located in Washington, D.C. the National Mall stretches over two miles from the U.S. Capitol on the east end to the Lincoln Memorial on the west end, with the Washington Monument towering in between. An impressive array of museums lines both sides of the mall, including the National Gallery of Art, the National Museum of Asian Art, the National Museum of African Art, the Hirshhorn Museum and Sculpture Garden, the U.S. Botanic Garden, the National Air and Space Museum, the National Museum of American History, the United States Holocaust Museum, the National Museum of the American Indian, the National Museum of African American History and Culture, and the National Museum of Natural History.

Arlington. — When we visit Washington, there are two other places which we should not fail to see. One of these is Arlington, situated about six miles from the city, south of the Potomac River. It is the old home of General Lee, the principal military leader of the Confederates. His temple-like house stands on a high eminence, from which the city of Washington is seen with all its beautiful buildings and monuments. But Arlington Cemetery holds a still greater interest. In this soldiers' cemetery are buried thousands upon thousands of the brave soldiers who fell during the Civil War and all wars since. The number of graves now totals over 400,000. As we look to the right and to the left of the mansion, we see thousands of little white headstones, each inscribed with the name of one of the fallen. Among them are larger monuments erected to generals and other high officers. One special monument is the Tomb of the Unknown Soldier, dedicated to American service members who died with their remains unidentified. We shall leave this place with a deep impression of the beauty of our national capital, and of the great sacrifices which have been made.

Mount Vernon. — The other place is Washington's home, Mount Vernon, which lies about ten miles below Arlington on the Potomac River. The place has changed very little since Washington lived there. We are transported over two hundred years back to the very beginning of our national life. The simplicity and dignity of the surroundings help us to understand the character of the first President. He himself is buried near his home, adjoining the gardens, where flowers are still blossoming as on the day of his death. Mount Vernon is, indeed, a national sanctuary where, from the memories of the past, we may get inspiration for the future.

QUESTIONS

1. Where was the first capital of the United States located? When removed, and where is its present location?

2. Name six of the most noted government buildings in Washington.

3. Why are Arlington and Mount Vernon famous?

4. Find out all you can about the Washington Monument — when built, what it commemorates, etc.

5. What is the District of Columbia?

CHAPTER XXVI

THE PRESIDENT

Importance of the Office. —The President of the United States is an official whose power is greater than that of a king. He is entrusted with this power on behalf of the people, and as the American nation grew stronger its President became more powerful and important in the world. Yet the President is not surrounded by any royal splendor or show of office. The earliest Presidents were simple in their manner of living, and the early traditions have been maintained. Though the Presidents no longer ride on horseback to their inauguration as Jefferson did, their mode of life is still very simple, and they avoid every unnecessary display of power and wealth.

The President's Daily Work. — The White House itself is a dignified but simple residence for the head of a nation. The White House consists of three major parts: the East Wing, the West Wing, and the Residence. The West Wing is the center of activity at the White House. In addition to housing offices of the President's top staff, it also includes the private office of the President, namely the Oval Office, and the Situation Room, where the most important interests of our nation are discussed and determined.

A visit to the President is most interesting. When the President receives visitors, the anteroom to the office is crowded with persons passing in and out. There are senators and representatives desirous of discussing impending legislation. There are diplomats bringing distinguished visitors from other countries. There are delegations of representative citizens from various parts of the country, who wish to urge upon the President some needed reform. In a short time the President meets all these people, listens to their wishes, and has a few cordial words for each one of the visitors.

The person of the President is protected at all times by secret service agents.

The work of the President requires ability of the highest order. The President must carry the most important matters in his or her mind and make decisions every day upon which the welfare of numberless people depend. The President must be a person of strong character, who will not be swayed by influence, but who will set before him or herself the one purpose of serving the nation and the people. The President must be able to say "No." It is desirable that the President should be a person of experience in public affairs, one whose character can be judged by what he or she has accomplished in other positions. Many successful presidents have been congressmen or senators for many years. Others have been governors. All these persons were conspicuous and well known by the American people, before they became Presidents.

The work of the President is arduous. From early morning until late at night, the responsibility of the office weighs on the mind of the President. Thousands of letters, texts, emails, and phone calls come to the White House urging upon the President action of one kind or another. All the departments of government are under the supervision of the President, and the President is in a measure responsible for the legislation which passes through Congress, and which ultimately is submitted to him or her for approval. So the President finds little leisure and rest. The responsibilities of this great office will be a strain on the strongest person. Few Presidents have lived long after their term of office has expired.

The Election of President. — The election of the President is carried on in a roundabout manner. The Constitution provides that at the time of the Presidential election each state shall choose a number of electors equal to its joint representation in the Senate and the House of Representatives. Some time after the election, the electors that have been chosen meet in the capital of the state and cast their votes for one individual for the office of President of the United States. These votes are then sent to Washington and counted in the presence of the Senate and House of Representatives. All these forms are observed at the present time, but as a matter of fact we typically know who has been chosen as soon as the November election day is over. The individuals who are nominated as Presidential electors on our party tickets have been pledged beforehand to vote for a certain candidate. They will not, therefore, vote for anyone else. We know that they will vote for Mr. Kennedy or Mr. Nixon, Mr. Romney or Mr. Obama. It has, therefore, been suggested that it would be better to abolish the electoral college altogether and have the people vote directly for the President and Vice-President. To do this it would be necessary to amend the Constitution.

Inauguration of President. — The President is installed in the office, or inaugurated, on the 20th of January following his election. The Inaugural ceremonies take place on the west front terrace of the Capitol. There are gathered the outgoing President and Vice-President, the justices of the Supreme Court, the senators and representatives, and many distinguished visitors, as well as a vast multitude of people on the National Mall awaiting the arrival of the President-elect and the Vice-President-elect. After the presidential party has arrived and all is quiet, the Chief Justice of the United States first administers the oath of office to the Vice-President. Then the Chief Justice administers the oath of office to the President, following which the new President delivers the inaugural address.

Immediately after the inaugural ceremony the President and Vice-President are guests of honor at a luncheon held by the leadership of the United States Congress held in Statuary Hall.

Then the presidential entourage proceeds up Pennsylvania Avenue to the White House, where it is customary for the president, vice-president, their respective families and leading members of the government and military to review the inaugural parade from an enclosed stand at the edge of the North Lawn. The parade, which proceeds along the 1.5 miles of Pennsylvania Avenue in front of the stand and the Front Lawn in view of the presidential party, features both military and civilian participants from all 50 states and the District of Columbia.

The President's Power. — The President has the general power of overseeing the work of the various executive departments of the government. It is the President's duty to see that the laws are faithfully executed. To this end the President must not only instruct the officials and issue regulations to them; but, should the laws be opposed in any locality, it is incumbent on the President to enforce them, if necessary, through the military power of the nation.

Appointing Officers. — The President has the right to appoint over 1200 of the most important officials of the federal government. Subordinate officials are appointed by the heads of the departments. The President appoints cabinet secretaries, heads of departments, and diplomatic officials. Such appointments must be submitted to the Senate, and that body must confirm them before they become valid. It is, therefore, a common practice for the President to consult the Senate before nominating any person for a very important office.

Making Treaties. — The President has the authority to negotiate treaties and to receive foreign ministers and ambassadors. He thus has a great influence upon our relations with foreign countries. It often depends upon the President whether this country shall sustain friendly relations with other nations or whether it shall incur the danger of war. The President is Commander in Chief of the U.S. Armed Forces: the Army, the Navy, the Air Force, the Coast Guard, and the Marine Corps. The President directs where troops shall be stationed, where ships shall be sent, and how weapons shall be used. All military generals and admirals take their orders from the president.

President's Messages. — The President has the right to address Congress on legislation and to urge upon the national legislators such changes in the laws as are considered wise. For this end, the President delivers an annual message as well as special messages. It is not intended that the President should take a further personal part in legislation. When the attention of Congress has been called to certain needs, it is for that body to consider the manner in which they may be met.

Veto Power. — When an act has been passed, as is the case in the States, it must be submitted to the President, who has the right to veto it. If a bill is sent to the Oval Office during the last ten days of a session, the President need not return it to Congress with his signature or veto. If the President does not sign it, the act fails and does not become a law. This is called the pocket veto. Acts sent to the President before this time must either be vetoed or signed and returned to Congress. That body has the right to pass a bill over the President's veto if two thirds of the members are in favor of doing so.

Presidential Succession. — In case of the death or disability of the President, the Vice-President becomes President. If the latter dies or becomes disabled, the law provides that the Speaker of the House shall act as President. Next in line are the Senate President Pro Tempore, the Secretary of State, the Secretary of the Treasury, the Secretary of Defense, and the Attorney General, and so on through the rest of the cabinet secretaries.

QUESTIONS

1. What other countries are republics?

2. How many Presidents has the United States had? Which of them died in office?

3. What offices did the last three Presidents hold prior to their election to the Presidency?

4. Compare present inaugural ceremonies today with those in Washington's and Jefferson's time.

5. Which Presidents have held prominent military offices?

6. What is the electoral college?

7. Tell how a President is elected.

8. Describe the inauguration of a President.

9. What appointive powers has the President?

10. What are the purposes of the messages sent

to Congress by the President? Find a copy of one and discuss it briefly.

11. Describe the veto power of the President.

12. Who becomes President if the President dies or becomes disabled?

13. Name two instances when this has been necessary.

CHAPTER XXVII

THE CABINET

Heads of Departments. — In the work of administering the affairs of the nation, the President is assisted by the cabinet. This council is composed of the heads of the great executive departments. These officials are appointed by the President and are responsible to him or her. If dissatisfied with their conduct, the President may call upon them to resign. We have already considered the work which is performed by some of these departments, but it will be well to review them in this place, as they are so important.

The Secretary of State. — The Secretary of State administers the foreign affairs of the nation. This cabinet member controls the actions of our diplomatic representatives abroad as well as of the consular officials. It is also the Secretary's duty to preserve important state documents and the original copies of the laws, to which the great seal of the United States is affixed. In the library of this department we may see such precious documents as the original copy of the Declaration of Independence and of the Constitution of the United States.

The Secretary of the Treasury. — The Secretary of the Treasury administers the financial department of the government. This cabinet member oversees the manufacturing of coins, the printing of money, the collection of taxes, the borrowing of money, and the distribution of funds to the various departments which are to expend them.

The Secretary of Defense. — The Secretary of Defense oversees all branches of the armed forces, which includes the Air Force, Army, Coast Guard, Marine Corps, and Navy. The Department of Defense, the government's largest agency, is headquartered at the Pentagon in Arlington, Virginia.

The Attorney General. — The Attorney General, as head of the Department of Justice, oversees the enforcement of the laws of the U.S. government. He or she also serves as the legal adviser of the government. Whenever an important action that may have legal consequences is to be taken, the President or other high officials confer with the Attorney General. The FBI, the DEA, and the U.S. Marshall Service are some of the departments under the oversight of the Attorney General.

The Secretary of the Interior. — Under the charge of the Secretary of the Interior are such interests as protection of public lands, conservation of natural resources, and preservation of wildlife throughout the nation, as well as overseeing relations with Native Americans.

The Secretary of Agriculture. — The Secretary of

Agriculture oversees the Department of Agriculture, more commonly known as the USDA. This department is responsible for ensuring the safety of food, safeguarding the nation's food supply, and conservation of agricultural land. It supports farmers through educational programs and financial assistance.

The Secretary of Commerce. — The Secretary of Commerce heads the Department of Commerce whose main purpose is to create jobs, promote economic growth, encourage sustainable development and improve standards of living for all Americans. Among its tasks are gathering economic and demographic data for business and government decision-making, and helping to set industrial standards. It also includes the Census Bureau which conducts the U.S. Census every ten years.

The Secretary of Labor. — The Secretary of Labor provides oversight to the Department of Labor which is responsible for making sure that the United States has a strong work force. This department focuses on the welfare of the wage earners: improving working conditions, combating discrimination in the workplace, ensuring adequate wage standards, work-related benefits and rights, job training, and unemployment insurance.

The Secretary of Health and Human Services. — The Secretary of Health and Human Services supervises the Department of Health and Human Services which is tasked with protecting the health of all Americans and providing essential human services. It is the department that manages the Medicare and Medicaid programs, and serves as home for the Surgeon-General. The Centers for Disease Control, the Food and Drug Administration, and the National Institutes of Health also operate under this department.

The Secretary of Housing and Urban Development. — The Secretary of Housing and Urban Development provides oversight to the Department of Housing and Urban Development, also known as HUD. HUD works to strengthen the housing market, to bolster the economy and protect consumers, to meet the need for quality affordable rental homes, to utilize housing as a platform for improving quality of life, and to build inclusive and sustainable communities free from discrimination.

The Secretary of Transportation. — The Department of Transportation with this Secretary as its head, works to ensure a fast, safe, efficient, accessible, and convenient transportation system that meets our vital national interests and enhances the quality of life of the American people, today and into the future. In addition to overseeing highways, railroads, ports, and air travel, this department provides some funding for mass transit projects.

The Secretary of Energy. — The Secretary of Energy supervises the Department of Energy, also known as DOE. Its responsibilities include domestic energy production, energy conservation, energy policy, and energy-related research. The DOE sponsors more research in the physical sciences than any other federal agency. The majority of this research is conducted through its system of National Laboratories.

The Secretary of Education. — The primary functions of the Department of Education, with this Secretary at its head, are to administer and coordinate most federal assistance to education, collect data on U.S. schools, and to enforce federal educational laws regarding privacy and civil rights. Its mission is to promote student achievement and preparation for global competitiveness by fostering educational excellence and ensuring equal access.

The Secretary of Veterans Affairs. — The Secretary of Veterans Affairs coordinates the efforts of the Department of Veterans Affairs in providing comprehensive healthcare services to eligible military veterans at VA medical centers and outpatient clinics located throughout the country. In addition, this department offers several other types of benefits, including disability compensation, vocational rehabilitation, education assistance, home loans, and life insurance. Lastly, it provides burial and memorial benefits to eligible veterans and family members at 135 national cemeteries.

The Secretary of Homeland Security. — The Secretary of Homeland Security supervises the Department of Homeland Security in its anti-terrorism work, as well as in its other functions: border security, immigration and customs, cyber security, and disaster prevention and management. This department, created in response to the September 11 attacks, is the most recently created cabinet department.

Civil Service. — In these various departments over two and a half million officials and clerks are employed. With the exception of the highest positions, which are filled by presidential appointment, the majority of civil service positions are classified as competitive service, meaning employees are selected based on merit after a competitive hiring process for positions that are open to all applicants. Most of these federal government jobs are filled through a competitive examination of the applicant's background, work experience, and education. Today only a small percentage of the jobs require a civil service examination.

QUESTIONS

1. Name the present members of the cabinet, and ascertain what public positions they held before being appointed to their present position.

2. What are some of the advantages of the civil service method of selecting public officers?

3. Name the departments of the cabinet in the order of their importance and value to the country.

4. By whom are the cabinet members appointed?

5. Are the members always chosen from the same political party which the President represents? Is this right?

CHAPTER XXVIII

THE CONGRESS

Congress. — The Congress of the United States is composed of the Senate and the House of Representatives. When we speak of a congressman or congresswoman, we refer to a member of the House. A member of the Senate is always spoken of as a senator.

Senators. — In the Senate of the United States each state, no matter how large or small, has two representatives. Rhode Island and Alaska are on a perfect equality in the Senate. The Senate, therefore, is not a very large body. There are one hundred senators, and they come to know each other very well. Senators are elected for a term of six years, but as they are frequently reelected it has happened that senators have held their office for as long as twenty or thirty years. The senators are elected directly by the people.

Congressmen and Congresswomen. — The members of the House of Representatives are also elected directly by the people. Each state is divided into congressional districts according to its population. California, the most populous state, has 53 districts, the smallest states have only one. At the present time the House of Representatives has 435 members. The representatives hold office for two years only, but are also frequently reelected. The House being a much larger body than the Senate, its members do not become so well acquainted with one another. The members who have held office longest acquire great influence.

The Speaker. — One of the representatives is elected Speaker of the House. The Speaker appoints all the standing and select committees. Through the committee on rules the Speaker arranges the business of the House. In this way the Speaker determines what legislation shall be taken up and how much time shall be given to each measure. No member is permitted to speak unless that person is recognized by the Speaker, and as the Speaker cannot recognize all who desire to speak, it follows that the Speaker has the power to select the persons who will be permitted to be heard on the floor of the House. A member of the House can, therefore, accomplish very little if the Speaker is opposed to him or her. Members of long service in the House will be made chairpersons of the important committees. The Speaker will consult with these individuals upon legislation. In this way the policy of the House is determined.

The Vice-President. — The Senate is presided over by the Vice-President of the United States. The Vice-President is not a member of the Senate, and has no vote unless the senators are equally divided in opinion in which case the vote of the Vice-President decides the question. While in the House the members are strictly limited in the time given to them for speaking, it is different in the Senate. The Standing Rules of the

United States Senate provide that no senator may make more than two speeches on a motion or bill on the same legislative day. The length of these speeches is not limited by the rules, so in most cases, senators may speak for as long as they please. Often, the Senate adopts unanimous consent agreements imposing time limits. In other cases, such as in the Budget process, limits are imposed by statute. In general, however, the right to unlimited debate is preserved, so a senator may speak at length on any measure before the Senate. It has happened that senators have talked so long against a certain bill that the session ended before the bill could be passed. This is called "talking a bill to death."

Bills. — As in the state legislatures, every bill which is introduced must be referred to a committee. It cannot be acted upon until the committee has reported. Many thousands of bills are never reported upon, but, as we say, they die in the committee room or they are put to sleep there. Committees invite certain individuals to testify before them. Most individuals respond favorably to an invitation to testify, believing it to be a valuable opportunity to communicate and publicize their views on a question of public policy. However, if a person will not come by invitation alone, a committee may require an appearance through the issuance of a subpoena.

All bills for the purpose of raising revenue, that is, for imposing or changing taxes, must first be introduced in the House. The Senate may amend such bills when they come to it, so that it also exercises a great power over the revenues. The Senate has also the right to give or refuse its consent to any treaty which the President has negotiated with a foreign country. Thus, it comes about that the Senate exerts a great influence over our foreign affairs. Without the approval of the Senate it is impossible for the President to make a treaty or to appoint certain diplomatic officials.

QUESTIONS

1. Describe the appearance of the Senate chamber, or of the hall of the House of Representatives.

2. Name six prominent senators and six members of the House.

3. Why do the members of the House submit to the power of the Speaker?

4. Who is the member of Congress for the district in which you live? What was his or her profession being before elected to Congress?

5. Does it seem just that California or New York should have no more senators than Rhode Island or Delaware?

6. How many members has the Senate now? The House of Representatives?

7. Are the territories represented in Congress?

8. What do we mean by an allowance for mileage? By the franking privilege?

9. How and for how long is a senator elected?

10. In case of the death of a senator, how is his or her successor chosen?

11. How many congressional districts in your state? Why?

12. When does a treaty negotiated by the President become a law?

13. When can the President of the Senate vote?

14. Why should all bills for the raising of revenue originate in the House? What power has the Senate regarding such bills?

CHAPTER XXIX

THE FEDERAL COURTS

Powers of the Courts. — The courts of the federal government are of great dignity and authority. The entire government is carried on under the Constitution, but the courts have the power to decide as to the meaning of any constitutional provision. Congress has the right to legislate, but its action must be limited by the powers granted in the Constitution. If it goes beyond these powers in the opinion of the Supreme Court, the court will declare its action unconstitutional. A decision of this kind would render the act void, because whatever law the courts do not approve has no validity.

District and Circuit Courts. —The lowest federal court is the district court. There is one such tribunal in every state and the District of Columbia, and the larger states have two or more. The next higher court is the circuit court. From both of these tribunals cases can be taken to the circuit court of appeals. There are 13 such courts in the United States. The circuit court of appeals is composed of three judges. The official who carries out the decrees and judgments of a federal court is called the marshal. In the case of the state courts this duty is performed by the sheriff.

The Supreme Court. — Any case involving the question whether a law or an official act is valid under the Constitution may be taken to the Supreme Court of the United States. This is also true in certain criminal cases involving life and liberty. The Supreme Court is composed of nine justices who are lawyers of great ability. The court is a body of impressive dignity. When it is in session, the judges wear judicial gowns, which add to their aspect of gravity. The ablest attorneys from all parts of the nation appear before this court to argue cases.

Jurisdiction. —The federal courts hear cases which arise under the federal Constitution or under the laws passed by Congress. Ordinary criminal cases are tried in the courts of the state. If a person should steal timber from a federal forest reserve, he would be tried before a federal court. Ordinary lawsuits between citizens also come up before the state courts. But if we are suing a citizen of another state, we may bring our action either in a court of his state or in a federal court. In such cases the federal courts are usually appealed to. Federal courts also hear all cases relating to navigation on the large rivers, lakes, and the sea.

Appointment of Judges. — The judges in all the federal courts are appointed by the President with the consent of the Senate. They are not appointed for a definite term, but during good behavior. This means that they hold office for life, unless they should be guilty of some crime or misdemeanor. In that case they may be deprived of their office, after being impeached by the House and found guilty by the Senate. Other high officials, including the President, may be impeached and tried in a similar manner. Only two Presidents have been impeached, and both were acquitted by the Senate. To pronounce a judge or official guilty, the votes of at least two thirds of the senators are required.

QUESTIONS

1. Is it better that judges should be elected for a limited time, or appointed for life?

2. For what crimes could a marshal make arrests?

3. Name the present justices of the Supreme Court. Did they hold judicial office before coming to their present positions?

4. What should be the character and attainments of a Supreme Court Justice?

5. What powers has the Supreme Court?

6. Why is it necessary to have such a body?

7. Name one law passed by Congress which the Supreme Court has declared unconstitutional.

8. What are district and circuit courts?

9. In what court would a postmaster accused of embezzling government money be tried? Why?

10. If you were injured in another state and brought suit to recover damages, where and in what courts could the case be tried?

CHAPTER XXX

INTERNATIONAL ORGANIZATIONS

Although our state and nation are very powerful, they necessarily have relations with other countries. No nation is entirely self-sufficient. They must all cooperate in order that the greatest advantages of civilization may be secured. Thus, nations help one another in gaining important information, in protecting one another against epidemics, in forwarding one another's mail, and in making it possible to have commercial intercourse. For these various purposes international organizations have been created, many of which have the United States as a member.

Every international organization has a central office. Some of these are located in Switzerland, some in Belgium, some in other countries. This central bureau supplies all the governments with information about the matters with which it deals. It also helps the various governments to transact their business with one another.

The United Nations. — The most important international organization is the United Nations, otherwise known as the UN. The United Nations seeks to promote international co-operation and to create and maintain international order. It was established in 1945 after World War II in order to prevent another such global conflict. At its founding, the UN had 51 member states; there are now 193. The headquarters of the UN is in New York City, with other offices in Geneva, Nairobi, and Vienna.

The organization is financed by assessed and voluntary contributions from its member states. Its objectives include maintaining international peace and security, promoting human rights, fostering social and economic development, protecting the environment, and providing humanitarian aid in cases of famine, natural disaster, and armed conflict. The UN is the largest, most familiar, most internationally represented and most powerful intergovernmental organization in the world.

The Security Council. — The United Nations Security Council (UNSC) is one of the six principal organs of the United Nations, charged with the maintenance of international peace and security as well as accepting new members to the UN and approving any changes to the UN charter. Its powers include the establishment of peacekeeping operations, the establishment of international sanctions, and the authorization of military action through Security Council resolutions; it is the only UN body with the authority to issue binding resolutions to member states.

The Security Council consists of fifteen members.

The great powers that were the victors of World War II—the Soviet Union (now represented by Russia), the United Kingdom, France, Republic of China (now represented by the People's Republic of China), and the United States—serve as the body's five permanent members. These permanent members can veto any substantive Security Council resolution, including those on the admission of new member states or candidates for Secretary-General. The Security Council also has 10 non-permanent members, elected on a regional basis to serve two-year terms. The body's presidency rotates monthly among its members.

Security Council resolutions are typically enforced by UN peacekeepers, military forces voluntarily provided by member states and funded independently of the main UN budget.

The World Health Organization. — The World Health Organization, also known as WHO, is a specialized agency of the UN that is concerned with international public health. Established in 1948, it is headquartered in Geneva, Switzerland. Since its creation, it has played a leading role in the eradication of smallpox. Its current priorities include reduction of spread of communicable diseases, in particular HIV/AIDS, Ebola, malaria and tuberculosis; the mitigation of the effects of non-communicable diseases; nutrition, food security and healthy eating; occupational health; and substance abuse.

The International Criminal Court. — The International Criminal Court, also known as ICC, is an intergovernmental organization and international tribunal that sits in The Hague in the Netherlands. The ICC has the jurisdiction to prosecute individuals for the international crimes of genocide, crimes against humanity, and war crimes. The ICC is intended to complement existing national judicial systems and it may therefore only exercise its jurisdiction when certain conditions are met, such as when national courts are unwilling or unable to prosecute criminals or when the UN Security Council or individual nations refer situations to the Court. Currently, 124 states are party to the Rome Statute, which governs the operation of the ICC, and therefore are members of the ICC.

The International Monetary Fund. — The International Monetary Fund, also known as the IMF, is an international organization headquartered in Washington, D.C. Its members include "189 countries working to foster global monetary cooperation, secure financial stability, facilitate international trade, promote high employment and sustainable economic growth, and reduce poverty around the world." The IMF while working to improve the economies of its member countries also plays a central role in the management of international financial crises.

The World Bank. — The World Bank is an international financial institution that provides loans to countries of the world for capital programs. It is headquartered in Washington, D.C. and works closely with the IMF.

The Group of Twenty. — The Group of Twenty,

also known as G20, is an international forum for the governments and central bank governors from 20 major economies. Currently, these are Argentina, Australia, Brazil, Canada, China, France, Germany, India, Indonesia, Italy, Japan, Mexico, Russia, Saudi Arabia, South Africa, South Korea, Turkey, United Kingdom, United States, and the European Union. Founded in 1999, the G20 aims to discuss policy issues relating to international financial stability. It seeks to address issues that go beyond the responsibilities of any one organization. The G20 heads of government or heads of state have periodically conferred at summits since their initial meeting in 2008. The group also hosts separate meetings of finance ministers and foreign ministers due to the expansion of its agenda in recent years.

The North Atlantic Treaty Organization. — The North Atlantic Treaty Organization, also known as NATO, is an intergovernmental military alliance between 29 North American and European countries based on the North Atlantic Treaty signed in 1949. NATO constitutes a system of collective defense whereby its member states agree to mutual defense in response to an attack by any external party.

QUESTIONS

1. What are international organizations? Why necessary? Name six.

2. Describe the function of the World Health Organization.

PART IV

Some American Ideals

CHAPTER XXXI

HOSPITALITY
TO ALL PEOPLE

The city of New York has one of the most beautiful harbors in the world. If we were to enter it on one of the big ocean steamers, we should see to our left the green, wooded hills of New Jersey, and the high forts of Governor's Island. To our right would stretch the level shore of Long Island, with its many towns, to which people resort in the summer. Ahead would rise the tall, tower-like buildings of the city of New York, which is connected with Brooklyn by the wonderful sweep of the high Brooklyn Bridge. But there, as we enter the harbor, on a small island arises the Statue of Liberty, enlightening the world. This is a tall figure of a woman holding in her hand high above her head a torch, which at night sheds light over the entire harbor. This great statue was presented to the people of the United States by our Sister Republic, France. It was placed here at the gateway of our country so that all who come from other countries may realize that they are entering the land of freedom.

Many thousand ships pass into this harbor every

year. They carry in their holds great quantities of goods which our merchants have purchased in other countries. They bring lace and silks from France, objects of art from Italy, clothing of various kinds from England and Germany, coffee from Brazil, rubber and gold from Africa. But they bring a more precious freight than all this. On these ships return to our shores many thousands of our countrymen who have been traveling in foreign lands on business, to study, to learn the customs of other nations, or for health or pleasure. With them come thousands and thousands of people who have never been in this country before. From all parts of the world they come, anxious to make their home in our rich country and to share with us the blessings of freedom and good government. Over a million immigrants have come to our shores in a single year. Many years ago most of them came to New York, but other ports, like Boston, Baltimore, Philadelphia, Charleston, New Orleans, San Francisco, and Seattle, were also doorways through which strangers entered our land. In the 18th and 19th centuries, they used to come mostly from England, Ireland, and Germany, but starting in the 20th century more people came from other regions, including Russia, Eastern Europe, and Asia. Today 40% of our immigrants come from the Americas, 40% from Asia, with the remaining 20% from other areas of the world. Almost all of them arrive by air.

When the immigrants of old reached the harbor of New York, they were very happy that the long voyage was over. They may have had to travel many days by railway in Europe before they came to the port at which they took their ship. Then came the ocean voyage of ten days or two weeks, with nothing to look at but the sea and the sky. They had left home and dear ones behind. They came in order that they and their children might lead a happier and freer life in this country. In their old home, they may have had to work sixteen hours a day for wages too low to enable them to live in comfort. For years they saved every penny in order to be able to pay their passage to the new country, where men were free and equal. And now their hopes were at last being fulfilled and they reached the end of their voyage.

When they reached the port of New York, however, they were not at once allowed to go on shore; they were not immediately welcomed and taken care of by kind friends. Instead, all immigrants were taken to Ellis Island, where the officials of the government inspected them to make sure that they were able-bodied individuals. Upon passing the inspection, they took their big bundles of baggage and were transferred by steamer or ferry to a railway station, where they began their journey to their final destination.

Nowadays most people from other countries arrive by air, scattering immediately all over our broad land.

Many of these millions of people who come to us from foreign lands soon become Americans; they learn our language and learn to love our government and institutions. If they work hard and are thrifty, they soon better their condition. They are able to have their own homes and to save a little money against sickness or old age. Their children will go to school, and will enjoy all the opportunities our country offers. As they become better educated, their life becomes more enjoyable, and many among them acquire wealth and influence.

Our nation welcomes people from all the countries of the world. Our nation is thus composed of people from a variety of traditions, and all the good and noble qualities which they bring will enrich our national life. They represent time-honored civilizations from which we have much to learn. They bring to our shores not only able hands, but willing minds.

CHAPTER XXXII

LIBERTY

If we look at one of our old silver coins, the quarter or half-dollar, we shall see on it the head of a woman. She wears a diadem, or head-band, on which is written the word "Liberty." On her head she wears a curious cap, which is called the cap of liberty. This has the same form as the cap which in old Rome a master gave to a slave whom he set free. It was the sign of freedom, and it has remained so till this day, although happily there are no more slaves to be freed. We also often write the word "Liberty" on our banners and carve it in stone on our public buildings. All this shows what we think of it. When our forefathers had braved a harsh climate, when they had made themselves homes in the American wilderness, when they had cleared the land around their villages and made the earth bear rich crops, when they had built towns and had made fleets of ships to sail on the sea, then they felt that they wanted liberty. They wanted to manage their own affairs and not to be subject to a government across the ocean. So they bravely fought the armies of England and suffered great hardships until they had finally won that liberty which they wanted and which was their right.

That is one form of liberty, for a people to be free and independent of control by an outside government, which they did not elect. At that time our nation was still small, having fewer people than the one state of Kansas has at present. But our forefathers knew that we could become a great and powerful nation, if our people were allowed to govern themselves. So they risked their lives and their all to secure so desirable an end. Liberty, however, means more than freedom from foreign rule. It is not enough that no outside government should be able to control us. Suppose some man should gather an army about himself and should make himself so powerful that he could force us to do what he pleased. Even if he were an American, we should not be free if we had to obey him. This is what Napoleon did in France. He was a lieutenant in the army, and when there was an uprising of the people in Paris, he commanded his gunners to fire their cannon into the crowd. This act restored order, but it also gave Napoleon the start in his struggle for power. He finally got control of the army, and his will was law in France. He even made war on the neighboring nations and conquered some of them. He desired to be the ruler of the world. That purpose he did not attain. Government by a Napoleon is not liberty. Liberty means that the nation is governed by the persons whom it has freely elected. So our forefathers adopted the Constitution. In all the states, too, constitutions were made. These provide that the President and the governors and the legislatures shall be elected by the people. This is what we call political liberty.

Some people think that if they live in a land of

liberty they ought to be able to do exactly what they please, without being hindered by any one. Would it be liberty to throw stones at a neighbor's windows, or to use firearms in the main streets, or to drive an automobile so fast as to endanger life? No; liberty does not mean that we can do anything we please. If we are to live in peace and harmony with our fellow-citizens, we must respect their rights. Imagine for a minute what would happen if every one did as he or she liked. The community would be at the mercy of the criminal classes. Not only would property be insecure, but life itself would be in danger. But that would not be liberty it would be anarchy. If there were no restraint, there would be no liberty. So we have laws which protect us from violence, and force us to respect the rights of others. To obey such laws is not to sacrifice freedom, because if people did not obey them, no one would be free.

We do want to be free to do what we choose, as long as we do not injure any one else. We often hear people say, "This is a free country." That does not mean that we have no laws which every one must obey. It means that we have no unnecessary laws. In some countries, people are not allowed to follow the business which they like. This is not liberty. In others, the police are always watching people, opening their letters, and giving them orders. Neither is this liberty. Sometimes the government is overly careful to protect people against their own carelessness. In our country, we may walk on the railway tracks, or jump on a train when it is beginning to move, or ride a bicycle in crowded streets. We take the risk of injury ourselves. In some countries, these things are forbidden because they are dangerous.

It is not difficult to do what the law demands. If we do not do things which injure others, we are free to go where we please and to follow our own wishes. We are truly free when we do what is right, because then we shall live happily and without fear. If we wrong others, or if we do that which is low and mean, we shall ourselves become low and mean, and our happiness will be at an end. So liberty, and good laws, and self-respect, and respect for the rights of other people are all one. We are free if all do what is right.

CHAPTER XXXIII

EQUALITY OF OPPORTUNITY

It is impossible that all persons should have the same amount of money and property. We cannot have such equality and do not want it. A person who has worked harder, or has learned his or her business or trade better, or does more for his fellow-citizens than others do, deserves better payment. But the equality which we believe in is that all persons should have an equal chance to do all that their abilities will let them do. Now in some countries, a boy must follow the trade of his father, even if he does not like it and can do something else better; or if he has no rich and powerful friends, a young man cannot get ahead in life. In our country, we do not ask who young persons' parents and grandparents are, but who they are themselves. We do not ask who is backing the young people, but what they have learned and what they can do. It is because every person has the whole world and every chance open before him or her that our country is so prosperous. We must see to it that this shall never be changed, for this is true equality.

The example of many great persons who began

life as poor boys or girls shows that in our country the highest honors may come to a person, even if that person has to start at the very bottom. Such honors, however, do not come to all. Not all of us, or most of us, attain to high honor as citizens, or to great wealth, but we are all equal in that we have an equal chance to use our powers and abilities. We may also be equal in happiness, for wherever people do their duty, whether as farmers or teachers, plumbers or bankers, they lead honorable lives. If they try to get what is not due them, if they are untrue, cruel, or afraid of work, they will have no honor, no matter how rich they may be. So in our country, though we cannot all be President, we can all do the work for which we are best fitted, and we shall be judged by the way in which we do our duty. When we say that our country is the land of equality, we mean this, that every person may make the most of his or her talents. The great opportunities that are open before all of us should inspire us to great effort.

It is because we believe in equality that we think so much of our schools. Unless all boys and girls can have at least a public school education, they do not get a fair start in life. Of course, there have been individuals who have done great things without ever going to school, but they were strong enough to give themselves the education which their parents could not give them. Fortunately, all children today do have the opportunity to attend school.

CHAPTER XXXIV

PATRIOTISM

The love of country has at all times been a powerful motive among those races that have achieved most in the world. The love of the Athenian for his native city, the pride of the Roman in the great Empire of which he was a member, have been inherited and developed by the citizen of the modern state. We love our country because it is our own. It is the field within which the action of our lives takes place, and its population is made up not only of our friends and close acquaintances, but of all the other people who stand for the ideas and customs which we ourselves cherish. Our nation is made one by its common memory of the great struggles which it has gone through and the triumphs which it has achieved. The history of our country is full of glorious deeds and great achievements. We love to dwell on the contest which the early settlers waged in the wilderness against the forces of nature. We follow with interest the upbuilding of communities and states. The great struggle in which our country claimed and maintained its independence fills us with enthusiasm. We love to read the lives of the great leaders, from Winthrop and Washington down to the statesmen of the present time, who have guided the nation in times of peace and of war.

Our nation has a common language and literature. Although many other languages are spoken, the one language is understood by all. Our nation has its own ideals of political life, which have already been set forth in these pages. We believe that the government should rest on public opinion, and that the will of every citizen should enter into the life of the state. We believe in peace and justice in international relations. In social life, too, our ideals are those of a new, rich, and hopeful country. We do not have classes of nobility or inherited privileges. It is our ideal that all persons should rely upon their own character and abilities, and that they should be given a free chance with every one else to show what they can do. Their success in life should depend upon the extent to which they have made themselves useful to their fellow citizens.

All these things together make the ideal of American nationality. The belief in this ideal, and the desire to realize and maintain it, is true patriotism. We cannot be truly patriotic without knowing and understanding what our national life means and what our nation stands for. When we thoroughly understand these ideals and devote ourselves to them, we are patriots. Patriotism is not a thoughtless feeling. When we hang out our national flag in front of our home, or when we cheer the patriotic sentiments of a public speaker, we should know that it is not merely a flag or the outward excitement that makes patriotism, but the deep feeling of devotion and sacrifice which lies back of such outward expressions.

One of the first things that occurs to us when we speak of patriotism is the readiness to sacrifice our welfare and even our life when the needs of our country require. Bravery in war is the most striking expression of patriotism. We pay special honor to those who have shown great courage at times when their country was endangered by invasion or by war. History is full of shining examples of persons who have given up every thought of self and have laid down their lives cheerfully in order to save their country. A teacher will be happy to tell the story of Leonidas, of Manlius, or of Winkelried. Our own history, too, has many examples of personal bravery. We need only refer to John Paul Jones, Ethan Allen, and the steadfast courage of Washington.

Patriotism is something positive and active,—a readiness to do something for our country. It does not express itself in a narrow-minded hostility to foreign people. It is not patriotic to think that all foreigners are inferior and that their countries are less advanced than ours. Such ideas only show ignorance. We are only one of the great nations, though we want to be and remain a great people. Our love for our own country should not express itself in enmity against others. A strong nation may well be friendly and just to other peoples, and protect the foreigners who have placed themselves under the care of its government. It would be a disgrace to our nation if foreigners were not protected as we ourselves expect to be when we find ourselves in foreign lands.

Though bravery in times of war excites our interest most, still citizens have need of bravery also in the quiet years of peace. They must be brave to do their own thinking, brave to act according to their sense of justice. If they hold office, they must be brave enough to face reproach and enmity for the sake of doing right and to disoblige powerful friends who might desire to influence their action in their own interest. It may even be said that it requires a greater and more persistent courage to fulfill our duty to our state in times of peace than in times of war. The excitement of war carries soldiers, as it were, outside of themselves. They are raised to a higher plane of courage and self-sacrifice. But in the ordinary times of peace, citizens have no such powerful incentive for devotion to the welfare of their country. They are surrounded by persons who are striving for their own interest. Each one, therefore, must constantly set before him or her the great things which our country stands for, and which our government must accomplish for the people if our nation is to prosper in the future.

To make our country safe and respected, a good home for ourselves and those that come after us, should be the desire of every patriotic citizen. A special duty is laid upon political leaders in our country. Here the people have a part in government. We aim at making the state the expression of the common life. It is not to exist for a favored few or for those in power and office-holders. Government is merely a service to the people of the nation. Ours is an experiment in popular government, which is being watched by all other nations. In order that it may succeed, we should all of us understand the nature of the high objects our nation is striving for. Every day of our lives we should assist in attaining these objects, even if we have to sacrifice time and money and opportunities. We should not begrudge our service, but should think it an honor and a privilege to assist in so great a work.

The great orator and patriot, Fisher Ames, has said: —

"What is patriotism? Is it a narrow affection for the spot where a man was born? Are the very clods where we tread entitled to this ardent preference because they are greener? No, sir, this is not the character of the virtue, and it soars higher for its object. It is an extended self-love, mingling with all the enjoyments of life, and twisting itself with the minutest filaments of the heart. It is thus we obey the laws of society, because they are the laws of virtue. In their authority we see, not the array of force and terror, but the venerable image of our country's honor. Every good citizen makes that honor his own, and cherishes it not only as precious, but as sacred. He is willing to risk his life in its defence, and is conscious that he gains protection while he gives it."

PART V

Federal Documents

CHAPTER XXXV

THE DECLARATION OF INDEPENDENCE

ADOPTED BY CONGRESS, JULY 4, 1776.

A DECLARATION BY THE REPRESENTATIVES OF THE UNITED STATES OF AMERICA, IN CONGRESS ASSEMBLED.

When, in the course of human events, it becomes necessary for one people to dissolve the political bands which have connected them with another, and to assume among the powers of the earth the separate and equal stations to which the laws of nature and of nature's God entitle them, a decent respect to the opinions of mankind requires that they should declare the causes which impel them to the separation.

We hold these truths to be self-evident, that all men are created equal; that they are endowed by their Creator with certain inalienable rights; that among these are life, liberty, and the pursuit of happiness; that, to secure these rights, governments are instituted among men, deriving their just powers from the consent of the governed; that, whenever any form of government becomes destructive of these ends, it is the right of the people to alter or abolish it, and to institute a new government, laying its foundation on such principles, and organizing its powers in such form, as to them shall seem most likely to effect their safety and happiness. Prudence, indeed, will dictate that governments long established should not be changed for light and transient causes; and, accordingly, all experience hath shown that mankind are more disposed to suffer, while evils are sufferable, than to right themselves by abolishing the forms to which they are accustomed. But when a long train of abuses and usurpations, pursuing invariably the same object, evinces a design to reduce them under absolute despotism, it is their right, it is their duty, to throw off such a government, and to provide new guards for their future security. Such has been the patient sufferance of these Colonies; and such is now the necessity which constrains them to alter their former systems of government. The history of the present king of Great Britain is a history of repeated injuries and usurpations, all having in direct object the establishment of an absolute tyranny over these States. To prove this, let facts be submitted to a candid world:—

He has refused his assent to laws the most wholesome, and necessary for the public good.

He has forbidden his governors to pass laws of immediate and pressing importance, unless suspended in their operations, till his assent should be obtained; and, when so suspended, he has utterly neglected to attend to them.

He has refused to pass other laws for the accommodation of large districts of people, unless those people would relinquish the right of representation in the legislature; a right inestimable to them, and formidable to tyrants only.

He has called together legislative bodies at places unusual, uncomfortable, and distant from the repository of their public records, for the sole purpose of fatiguing them into compliance with his measures.

He has dissolved representative houses repeatedly for opposing, with manly firmness, his invasions on the rights of the people.

He has refused, for a long time after such dissolutions, to cause others to be elected; whereby the legislative powers, incapable of annihilation, have returned to the people at large, for their exercise; the State remaining, in the mean time, exposed to all the dangers of invasions from without, and convulsions within.

He has endeavored to prevent the population of these States; for that purpose, obstructing the laws for the naturalization of foreigners; refusing to pass others to encourage their migration hither, and raising the conditions of new appropriations of lands.

He has obstructed the administration of justice by refusing his assent to laws for establishing judiciary powers.

He has made judges dependent on his will alone, for the tenure of their offices, and the amount and payment of their salaries.

He has erected a multitude of new offices, and sent hither swarms of officers, to harass our people, and eat out their substance.

He has kept among us, in times of peace, standing armies, without the consent of our legislature.

He has affected to render the military independent of, and superior to, the civil power.

He has combined with others to subject us to a jurisdiction foreign to our constitution, and unacknowledged by our laws; giving his assent to their acts of pretended legislation:—

For quartering large bodies of armed troops among us;

For protecting them, by mock trial, from punishment for any murders which they should commit on the inhabitants of these States;

For cutting off our trade with all parts of the world;

For imposing taxes on us without our consent;

For depriving us, in many cases, of the benefits of trial by jury;

For transporting us beyond seas to be tried for pretended offences;

For abolishing the free system of English laws in a neighboring province, establishing therein an arbitrary government, and enlarging its boundaries, so as to render it at once an example and fit instrument for introducing the same absolute rule into these Colonies;

For taking away our charters, abolishing our most valuable laws, and altering, fundamentally, the powers of our government;

For suspending our own legislatures, and declaring themselves invested with power to legislate for us in all cases whatsoever.

He has abdicated government here, by declaring us out of his protection, and waging war against us.

He has plundered our seas, ravaged our coasts, burned our towns, and destroyed the lives of our people.

He is at this time transporting large armies of foreign mercenaries to complete the works of death, desolation, and tyranny, already begun with circumstances of cruelty and perfidy scarcely paralleled in the most barbarous ages, and totally unworthy the head of a civilized nation.

He has constrained our fellow-citizens, taken captive on the high seas, to bear arms against their country, to become the executioners of their friends and brethren, or to fall themselves by their hands.

He has excited domestic insurrections amongst us, and has endeavored to bring on the inhabitants of our frontiers, the merciless Indian savages, whose known rule of warfare is an undistinguished destruction of all ages, sexes, and conditions.

In every stage of these oppressions, we have petitioned for redress in the most humble terms; our repeated petitions have been answered only by repeated injury. A prince whose character is thus marked by every act which may define a tyrant is unfit to be the ruler of a free people.

Nor have we been wanting in attentions to our British brethren. We have warned them, from time to time, of attempts by their legislature to extend an unwarrantable jurisdiction over us. We have reminded them of the circumstances of our emigration and settlement here. We have appealed to their native justice and magnanimity, and we have conjured them, by the ties of our common kindred, to disavow these usurpations, which would inevitably interrupt our corrections and correspondence. They, too, have been deaf to the voice of justice and of consanguinity. We must, therefore, acquiesce in the necessity, which denounces our separation, and hold them, as we hold the rest of mankind, enemies in war; in peace, friends.

We, therefore, the representatives of the UNITED STATES OF AMERICA, in general congress assembled, appealing to the Supreme Judge of the world for the rectitude of our intentions, do, in the name and by the authority of the good people of these Colonies, solemnly publish and declare, That these United Colonies are, and of right ought to be, *Free and Independent States;* that they are absolved from all allegiance to the British Crown, and that all political connection between them and the State of Great Britain is, and ought to be, totally dissolved; and that, as *Free and Independent States*, they have full power to levy war, conclude peace, contract alliances, establish commerce, and do all other acts and things which Independent States may of right do.

And for the support of this Declaration, with a firm reliance on the protection of DIVINE PROVIDENCE, we mutually pledge to each other our lives, our fortunes, and our sacred honor.

JOHN HANCOCK.

NEW HAMPSHIRE. — Josiah Bartlett, William Whipple, Matthew Thornton.

MASSACHUSETTS BAY. — Samuel Adams, John Adams, Robert Treat Paine, Elbridge Gerry.

RHODE ISLAND ETC. — Stephen Hopkins, William Ellery.

CONNECTICUT. — Roger Sherman, Samuel Huntington, William Williams, Oliver Wolcott.

NEW YORK. — William Floyd, Philip Livingston, Francis Lewis, Lewis Morris.

NEW JERSEY. — Richard Stockton, John Witherspoon, Francis Hopkinson, John Hart, Abraham Clark.

PENNSYLVANIA. — Robert Morris, Benjamin Rush, Benjamin Franklin, John Morton, George Clymer, James Smith, George Taylor, James Wilson, George Ross.

DELAWARE. — Cæsar Rodney, George Read, Thomas M'Kean.

MARYLAND. — Samuel Chase, William Paca, Thomas Stone, Charles Carroll of Carrollton.

VIRGINIA. — George Wythe, Richard Henry Lee,

Thomas Jefferson, Benjamin Harrison, Thomas Nelson, Jr., Francis Lightfoot Lee, Carter Braxton.

NORTH CAROLINA. — William Hooper, Joseph Hewes, John Penn.

SOUTH CAROLINA. — Edward Rutledge, Thomas Hayward, Jr., Thomas Lynch, Jr., Arthur Middleton.

GEORGIA. — Button Gwinnett, Lyman Hall, George Walton.

CHAPTER XXXVI

ANALYSIS OF THE UNITED STATES CONSTITUTION

(In this brief analysis there are indicated merely the most important of the provisions of the Constitution, with which every person ought to be familiar.)

I. ORGANIZATION OF THE GOVERNMENT

1. THE LEGISLATIVE DEPARTMENT.

The House of Representatives. — Members chosen every two years by such electors in the states as have the right to vote for members of the state legislature. Representatives must be twenty-five years of age, and must have been citizens for seven years. They are apportioned among the states according to population.

The Senate. — There are two senators from each state, elected for six years. One third of the members of the Senate are elected every two years. Senators must be thirty years of age, and must have been citizens for nine years. Each house is the judge of the election and qualifications of its own members. A majority constitutes a quorum to do business. Each house determines the rules of its proceedings, and keeps a journal. At the desire of one fifth of the members present, the yeas and nays on any question shall be entered on the journal.

2. THE EXECUTIVE DEPARTMENT. The President of the United States is elected by electors chosen by the voters in each state. Each state is entitled to as many electors as it has senators and representatives in Congress. The President must be a native-born citizen of the United States over thirty-five years of age. The Vice-President is elected in a similar manner.

3. THE JUDICIARY DEPARTMENT. — The Constitution provides for one Supreme Court. Inferior courts may from time to time be established by Congress. The judges shall hold office during good behavior. They are appointed by the President with the consent of the Senate.

II. THE POWERS OF THE FEDERAL GOVERNMENT

1. THE POWERS OF CONGRESS. — Congress may:—

Lay and collect taxes;

Borrow money;

Regulate commerce with foreign nations, and among the states;

Establish uniform laws on naturalization and on

bankruptcy;

Coin money;

Establish post-offices and post roads;

Grant patents and copyrights;

Define and punish offenses against international law;

Declare war;

Raise and support an army and a navy, and make rules for the land and naval forces;

Provide for calling forth the militia to execute the laws, and for the organization of the militia;

Exercise exclusive legislative power over the federal district (of Columbia) and other land and property of the United States;

Make all laws which shall be necessary and proper for carrying into execution these powers.

Congress may also admit new states into the Union, and may make all needful rules and regulations respecting the territories or other property belonging to the United States. All bills for raising revenue shall originate in the House of Representatives, but the Senate may propose amendments.

The House of Representatives further has the power to impeach or accuse any high official. The Senate shall try such impeachments. When the President of the United States is tried, the Chief Justice shall preside. The Senate further has the power to give or withhold its consent to all treaties and appointments made by the President.

2. THE EXECUTIVE. — The President is commander-in-chief of the army and navy.

He may require the opinion of the principal officer in each of the executive departments. (These officers form the President's cabinet.)

He may grant pardons for offenses against the United States.

He shall from time to time give the Congress information on the state of the Union (in his messages), and recommend measures of legislation.

He has the right to convene the houses of Congress in executive session.

He receives ambassadors and other foreign ministers.

He shall take care that the laws are faithfully executed.

By and with the consent of the Senate, the President makes treaties with foreign nations and appoints the higher public officials in the federal service.

3. THE FEDERAL COURTS. — The judicial power of the United States extends over the following matters:

All cases arising under the Constitution, the laws of the United States, and treaties;

Cases affecting ambassadors and other public ministers and consuls;

Cases of admiralty and maritime jurisdiction;

Controversies between two or more states, between a state and citizens of another state, and between citizens of different states;

Cases in which foreigners are a party. By the Eleventh Amendment, it is provided that the judicial power of the United States shall not extend to a suit prosecuted against a state by a citizen of another state or by a foreigner.

In all criminal trials there shall be a jury, and the trials shall be held in the state where the crime has been committed.

III. POWERS WHICH ARE DENIED TO THE UNITED STATES

The privilege of the writ of *habeas corpus* shall not be suspended, except in cases of rebellion or invasion.

No law shall be passed to punish a person for an action which was not a crime at the time when it was committed. Such a law would be called an *ex post facto* law.

Head taxes or other direct taxes shall not be laid unless in proportion to the population.

There shall be no tax on articles exported from any state.

No preference shall be given to the ports of one state over those of another, in the matter of commercial regulations.

No money shall be drawn from the treasury but in consequence of appropriations granted by law.

No title of nobility shall be granted.

The powers of the federal government are also limited by the Bill of Rights in the amendments, which see below.

IV. POWERS WHICH ARE DENIED TO THE STATES

States shall not enter into any treaty, alliance, or confederation.

They shall not coin money or issue bills of credit.

They shall not make anything but gold and silver coin legal tender for the payment of debts.

They shall not pass any *ex post facto* law or any law by which the obligation of existing contracts is impaired.

They shall not grant any title of nobility.

States shall not keep troops or ships of war in time of peace.

They shall not lay any duty on the tonnage of vessels.

The United States guarantees to every state in the Union a republican form of government. A state could not, therefore, under the Constitution, set up a monarchical government.

The United States also shall protect the states against domestic violence, on application of the legislature or of the executive of the state.

V. POWER OF AMENDMENT

The Constitution of the United States may be amended in the following manner: —

Amendments shall be proposed in either of the following ways: First, two thirds of both houses of Congress may propose amendments; second, on the application of the legislatures of two thirds of the states, a national convention for proposing amendments shall be called.

The amendments shall be ratified or adopted in either of the following ways: First, by the legislatures of three fourths of the several states; second, by conventions in three fourths of the states. Congress may determine which mode of ratification shall be used.

It is specially provided that no state shall, without its consent, be deprived of its equal representation in the Senate.

VI. THE BILL OF RIGHTS

The first ten amendments to the Constitution constitute the Bill of Rights.

Amendments. — I. Congress shall make no law establishing a religion, or prohibiting the free exercise thereof; it shall not abridge the freedom of speech or of the press, or of the right of the people peaceably to assemble and to petition the government.

II. The right of the people to keep and bear arms shall not be infringed.

III. No soldiers shall in time of peace be quartered in any house without the consent of the owner, nor in time of war except under law.

IV. The homes of the people shall not be searched, except upon warrants sworn to and describing particularly the place to be searched and the person or things to be seized.

V. In the trial of persons for crime, the due process of law shall be observed.

No person shall twice be tried for the same offense.

No person shall be compelled in a criminal case to be a witness against himself.

Private property shall not be taken for public use without just compensation.

The rights of a criminal to an impartial trial are further protected by Article VI.

VII. In suits at common law (civil cases) where the amount involved shall exceed $20, the right of trial by jury shall be preserved.

VIII. Excessive bail shall not be required, nor excessive fines be imposed, nor cruel and unusual punishments inflicted.

X. The powers not delegated to the United States by the Constitution, nor prohibited by it to the states, are reserved to the states respectively, or to the people.

XI. The power of federal courts is barred from hearing lawsuits against state governments brought by the citizens of another state or the citizens of a foreign country.

XII. Each elector must cast a vote for a President and a Vice-President on his or her ballot.

XIII. Neither slavery nor involuntary servitude shall exist except as a punishment for crime.

XIV. No state shall make or enforce a law which shall abridge the rights or immunities of citizens of the United States, nor shall it deny to any person within its jurisdiction the equal protection of the laws.

XV. The right of the citizens of the United States to vote shall not be denied on account of race, color, or previous condition of servitude.

XVI. Congress shall have the power to lay and collect taxes on income.

XVII. The Senate of the United States shall be composed of two senators from each state elected by the people thereof for six years, and each senator shall have one vote. In order to vote for a senator, a voter must be qualified to vote for members of the state legislature.

XVIII. The manufacture, sale, or transportation of intoxicating liquors within the United States for beverage purposes is prohibited.

XIX. The right of citizens of the United States to vote shall not be denied on account of sex.

XX. The terms of the President and Vice President shall end at noon on the 20th day of January, and the terms of Senators and Representatives at noon on the 3rd day of January, and the terms of their successors shall then begin.

XXI. The 18th Amendment is repealed. It becomes a federal offense to transport or import intoxicating liquors into U.S. states and territories where such transport or importation is prohibited by law.

XXII. No person shall be elected to the office of the President more than twice.

XXIII. Electors equal to the least populous state are granted to the District of Columbia.

XXIV. The right of citizens of the United States to vote in any election shall not be denied by reason of failure to pay any poll tax or other tax.

XXV. Procedures are established for filling vacancies in the offices of President and Vice-President.

XXVI. No law varying the compensation for the services of the Senators and Representatives shall take effect, until after the next election of Representatives.